Contents

Foreword

South African church leaders set out on a protest march to the South African parliament on February 29, 1988. The march was stopped before it reached its destination but this historic act thrust the Churches into the forefront of resistance to apartheid.

The church leaders were attempting to deliver a petition at the banning of 17 organisations campaigning for non-violent change in South Africa.

Since the march the situation in South Africa has deteriorated further. At the initiative of the British Council of Churches and Christian Aid, a large number of British-based organisations met to exchange views about what was happening and to share their concerns over British policy towards the region. As a result a major conference to debate Britain's position was convened in London on the first anniversary of the march in Cape Town.

This book is based on the arguments put forward at the conference. Part One scrutinises British Government policy towards southern Africa, spells out the new opportunities for negotiation and examines the economic measures which could underpin such negotiations if they are to herald the end of apartheid.

Part Two sets out the British Government's case and a further reply to it which stresses the urgent need for concerted international pressure from governments and business together.

It concludes with 'A Call to Action against Apartheid' which lists measures the British Government should implement.

Standing for the Truth has been possible because of the support of a wide range of organisations including:

Anti-Apartheid Movement
Catholic Institute for International Relations
Christian Concern for Southern Africa
Christian Ethical Investment Group
Council for World Mission
Methodist Church Division of Social Responsibility
United Reformed Church
United Society for the Propagation of the Gospel
World University Service

Introduction

It was at the end of the 18th century that people in Britain began to hear news of the Cape from the early missionaries. The reports were often of slavery.

One of those early reporters was Dr John Philip of the London Missionary Society. He wrote a book describing the brutality and repression. Prominent whites in the Cape sued him for libel.

He was convicted and fined. A collection was made in the churches here which more than met the fine. It was the first Defence and Aid Fund.

That was 170 years ago and the story of protest has continued. I quote this because the British Council of Churches (BCC) is not publishing *Standing for the Truth* on a sudden conversion or whim. We present it with confidence. It was prepared on the basis of many years' work and expresses the convictions which are held by nearly all the main Churches of this country.

When British governments had ultimate authority over South Africa, we did little to lift up the oppressed, either Boer or Black

---

It is presented at a time of great challenge and opportunity. Pressures of many sorts have led to the Namibian settlement and the fact that the Soviet Union and the United States are able to exert a common pressure in some of these conflicts is encouraging. The issue in southern Africa is not East versus West, but apartheid.

This is the moment when we need to press our own Government to take stronger action.

For we are implicated in the evil of apartheid. When British governments had ultimate authority over South Africa, we did little to lift up the oppressed, either Boer or Black.

5

British power was too often allied to overbearing white power, and so set a model for what was to follow. We too looked for cheap labour. We did little for black education.

In this century we have continued to exploit the commercial opportunities of a divided society.

In *Standing for the Truth*, the BCC is advocating that Britain should try and redress some of the wrongs. Together with Commonwealth and European Community partners, Britain should now plan and carry through political and economic measures to help bring about change in South Africa.

To suggest that a gentle, harmonious growth in prosperity will remove injustice is to forget the whole history of slavery

---

Such measures will bring pain. But, we must not forget the pain is there now. If you have read the affidavits of children in detention without charge, then you wonder what sort of pain can be worse.

It is doubtful whether a great evil can ever be cut out of a human society without pain. There is always a cry when the evil is exposed and attacked. To suggest that a gentle, harmonious growth in prosperity will remove injustice is to forget the whole history of slavery.

There will be no major economic developments unless the political future of the country is marked by the growth of social justice.

The steps the Government could take today are detailed in this book. In pressing this case I know we are dealing with matters of life and death. There are no easy answers. But a campaign of revolutionary violence and a martial law government are not a Christian alternative we can endorse.

Is a violent and bitter confrontation, broken lives, broken families, broken faith, all that is left? It is our Christian duty to develop the whole range of measures, short of violence, which will serve not to ameliorate apartheid but undermine its very existence.

The Rev Bernard Thorogood
Moderator of the Executive Committee of
British Council of Churches

PART ONE

The Way Forward

CHAPTER ONE

Southern Africa Today
– A Window of Opportunity

"We must emphasise from the start that it is the unprecedented seriousness of our present crisis, the enormity of the present suffering of the oppressed people of South Africa and the horrifying spectre of escalating violence that has led us to take our stand. Anyone who does not appreciate the untold daily sufferings of the people, the pain, the insecurity, the starvation and horrors of widespread unemployment will also not appreciate the need for drastic and extraordinary measures to put an end to all this misery as soon as possible."

Southern African Catholic Bishops' Conference, 1986

Since that bishops' statement, the repression and suffering inside South Africa has worsened. But, at the same time, a new window of opportunity has opened for international action to bring justice and peace to southern Africa. In Angola and Namibia, though not yet significantly at home, the South African Government has responded to international pressure. Improved relations between the Soviet Union and the West make concerted international pressure possible. This opportunity must be seized.

The background

By the mid-1980s, South Africa was in crisis. On the one hand, there was a vigorous and broad-based movement pressing for democracy. The United Democratic Front (UDF), born in 1983, mushroomed to embrace 700 organisations including students' groups, civic associations, churches, even sports clubs. Trade unions grew at an extraordinary speed, winning recognition agreements and members, and in 1985 forming a new Congress

LEFT:
Since the State of Emergency, thousands have been killed including many children. Six month-old Amanda Fanisi was asphyxiated by teargas fired by police.

of South African Trade Unions (COSATU) with an end to apartheid among its aims.

School boycotts won concessions, and the National Education Crisis Committee began to draft a new syllabus, aiming to replace the official curriculum in schools, subject by subject. In many townships, residents stopped paying rents to the municipality, claiming they did not represent the people, were inefficient and corrupt. In some areas, street committees formed the base of an alternative system of local authority. There was some conflict and division, but overall a heartening breadth and unity to the movement. There were signs both of the end of the old society and the seeds of a new one.

But Pretoria responded violently. From October 1984, troops were deployed in the townships. Figures are necessarily imprecise, but about 2,400 people were killed in the unrest between September 1984 and February 1987. There were frequent skirmishes; in 1985, in Langa, Crossroads, Queenstown and Mamelodi police opened fire indiscriminately into crowds.

UNICEF estimated that 140,000 children under the age of five died in 1986 as a consequence of war and destabilisation

---

A State of Emergency was declared in July 1985, with a daily average of 120 arrests and four deaths, during the first month. A second State of Emergency followed in June 1986, and has been in force ever since. Over 30,000 people have been detained, including many children. The primary targets for detention were UDF and COSATU leaders and supporters at a local level.

Pretoria was also wreaking havoc in the wider region. The military occupation of Namibia, confirmed illegal by the World Court in 1971, was effectively extended into southern Angola. In Mozambique, South Africa ignored its 1984 Nkomati Accord and continued to direct and supply the rebel Mozambique National Resistance (MNR), paralysing the economy. The MNR's methods were horrifically brutal. The United Nations International Children's Fund (UNICEF) estimated that 140,000 children under the age of five died in 1986 as a consequence of war and destabilisation in Angola and Mozambique. A series of South African military raids were launched into Botswana, Lesotho, Swaziland, Zambia and Zimbabwe. The railways to the sea were sabotaged, forcing the countries to depend on the longer routes through South Africa. By 1986, destabilisation was estimated to be costing the region US$8 billion per year. Not surprisingly, international pressure built up on Pretoria. For the first half of 1986, a group of seven Eminent Persons from the Commonwealth tried to promote a political dialogue aimed at replacing apartheid with democracy. But in June, they reported that the South African Government had moved consciously away from any realistic negotiating process. By the end of the year, the Commonwealth, the European Community, the United States and several other countries had all imposed new sanctions. Sir Geoffrey Howe, Britain's Foreign Secretary, attempted to restart negotiations but was brushed aside by Pretoria.

Repression

Today, the fundamental problem remains. As the US Deputy Secretary of State told the Senate Foreign Relations Committee in June 1988: "South Africa's governing elite remains steadfast in its determination to retain its monopoly on political power".

Yet the crisis is different. Above all, repression has intensified, as the Government attempts to silence the democratic resurgence of the early 1980s. On February 23 1988, the key organisations at the heart of the UDF, and of black consciousness groups, were forbidden to operate – there are now 32 groups banned. The November 1988 conviction of three UDF leaders and a South African Council of Churches worker suggests that it is high treason to work peacefully for the end of the present system of government. COSATU has been issued with a legal order to deal only with industrial, rather than political, matters. A new Labour Relations Amendment Act curbs the extent of the right to strike and outlaws solidarity actions. The Disclosure of Foreign Funding Bill gives the State the power to control the work of organisations, including churches, when that work is funded by foreign money. Roughly 1,500 people remained in detention at the end of 1988. Leaders who have been released are usually banned from political activity.

The same organisations also face a new range of illegal attacks. The head offices of COSATU, the South African Council of Churches and the Southern African Catholic Bishops' Conference have all been wrecked by fire bombs, as have various regional trade union and UDF-related buildings. Some local leaders have been assassinated. In a succession of townships, vigilante groups have emerged in opposition to UDF-related organisations. In Crossroads, KTC, KwaNdebele and around Pietermaritzburg, these groups have been allowed to fight without police intervention, or with mediators prevented from entering. Pro-government media portray the conflict as black fighting black, and use it as a warning of the

The primary targets for detention have been UDF and COSATU leaders and supporters.

consequences of introducing democracy. Yet there is ample evidence that vigilante groups and local township warlords are fostered and permitted by the State as a way of subduing genuinely democratic organisations.

The most sustained conflict has been in Natal, involving the Zulu cultural movement Inkatha. Inkatha is led by the Chief Minister of KwaZulu, Gatsha Buthelezi, and commands considerable support in KwaZulu, albeit in an atmosphere where party membership is a help in dealing with State authorities. Its policy has been one of dialogue with Pretoria, and it projects a moderate image overseas. However, the rise of UDF and COSATU in Natal was taken as a major challenge by Inkatha. A series of violent assaults were launched in the name of Inkatha on UDF supporters in the townships and hundreds of people have been killed and thousands wounded. Careful reviews of the evidence lay an overwhelming proportion of the blame for repeated instigations of violence at Inkatha's feet (see, for example, Mare and Hamilton, 1987). Church leaders have been active in seeking to end the conflict.

To suppress and to channel both the flow of information and debate, stringent reporting restrictions now apply to the press and foreign television coverage. A number of newspapers, including the *New Nation* established by the Catholic Bishops'

Conference, have been forced to suspend publication temporarily. Within South Africa, this distorts the picture of the true extent of conflict and of organisation, and removes vigilante groups from the public eye. In the same way, Pretoria controls the news transmitted to the outside world – the information on which the world forms judgments.

Reform

The overall picture is additionally complicated because Pretoria's policy combines repression with reform. The pass laws have been replaced by laws which permit people to stay in towns or on white farms if they have adequate housing – yet there is far too little housing, so these laws could be used to expel hundreds of thousands of people who previously did have rights of residence in towns or on farms. Money is to be spent on infrastructure, principally housing and electricity, for selected townships. Small business is to be encouraged, and some legislation restricting it (licences, health and safety, minimum wages) repealed. Funds for these programmes are to come, at least in part, from the privatisation of state industries. Facilities like public parks, and some urban housing areas, are no longer segregated by race (though the Conservative Party is seeking to reverse the trend).

Pretoria's approach to political reform rests largely on the new black councillors, however poor the turnout on which they were elected. Some will be invited to serve on Regional Service Councils (established to coordinate government services between 'white' areas and 'homelands' in a region), and on a proposed consultative National Council, joining representatives of other ethnic groups.

Yet "the so-called reforms are a sham whose purpose is to entrench the essentials of apartheid", wrote South Africa's four Roman Catholic archbishops in 1986. "Do not be deceived by

---

the programme of reform does not end apartheid but seeks to give it a less inhuman face

---

certain changes which have been made in South Africa," wrote 16 of the 21 Anglican bishops in August 1988, "The constitution is fundamentally racist. The Government continues to rule by clampdown and detentions. There is no meaningful freedom of speech nor opportunity for peaceful protest and democratic political organisation." The Commonwealth Eminent Persons concluded that the "programme of reform does not end apartheid but seeks to give it a less inhuman face. Its quest is power-sharing, but without surrendering overall white control."

The military option
When so many organisations were silenced in February 1988, church leaders concluded that the Government had chosen the 'military option' for South Africa. Repression and promotion of pliable alternative organisations are part of a recognised military strategy, known internationally as 'low intensity conflict'. The military objective is to manage conflict and wear down opposition, in an economically feasible way, and with a minimum of international headlines.

The crisis since 1984 has reinforced the already extensive role of the military in a highly centralised structure implementing both security and political policies. At the apex is the State Security Council, chaired by the State President with a general as secretary. Below are more than 500 regional, district and local Joint Management Centres (JMCs), composed of military, police and civilian officials usually chaired by a military officer. The JMCs coordinate the strategy of combined repression and reform.

The repression is intended to remove the present opposition leadership and popular organisations. The reform is intended to meet real economic needs, and so damp down the pressure for democracy. The JMCs are focusing infrastructure upgrading on specific townships, and especially on 34 where resistance has been most organised (including Alexandra in Johannesburg, and New Brighton outside Port Elizabeth). In the words of one general: "What is more important to the masses in the natural situation without revolutionary instigation is the economic and the social . . . and the Government is working towards giving them **in these fields** a better life." The derisory turnout in the October 1988 elections illustrates the problem of the strategy to date, but the Government sees it as a long-term process.

But for all the planning and strategy, the Government remains uncertain of its course. Reform measures such as relaxing the Group Areas Act are raised, rejected, raised again, watered down. Nelson Mandela's release is at one moment imminent, the next delayed. One speech calls for reform; the next insists to Afrikaanerdom that the interests of the Volk are safe in this Government's hands.

The democratic movement
The repression has undoubtedly succeeded in disrupting the extent of national organisation. The UDF is severely hampered at a national level, and legally restricted from organising.

Likewise, there is no national school students' organisation (above ground), nor national End Conscription Campaign for white conscientious objectors: both have been banned. In the first five months of 1988, strike action (in terms of person/days lost) was down to its 1986 level, 80% down on 1987. COSATU is having difficulty in bringing all of its regional offices into full operation.

Yet at a local level, the ferment has not been stopped. There are marked regional variations, and detentions and vigilantes have a debilitating impact, but opposition continues. Before its banning in February 1988, the youth organisation SAYCO was linking some 800 local youth groups, most of which still exist. The student boycott in the Western Cape in April 1988, involving tens of thousands of students, was the biggest since 1985. Women's organisations, prevented from holding mass meetings, are concentrating on local groups. Trade union membership continues to grow (the one major exception was the National Union of Mineworkers which lost 50,000 members after its 1987 strike, but it is now making up the loss).

Even at a national level, organisation is re-emerging all the time. COSATU has managed to hold a national conference, maintain its voice on political issues and call the largest ever national stay-away from work, a three day protest at the bannings.

Pretoria's policy combines repression with reform – above, police confront striking bread workers.

FOLLOWING PAGES:
The cornerstone of apartheid is forced removals to the homelands. Families are dumped in these rural areas with little land, few jobs and few basic services.

15

Marc Vanappelghem

The African National Congress (ANC) remains a magnet, with its exiled leaders meeting white opposition and business leaders, and even Afrikaaner rugby administrators. One of the most significant meetings was between the ANC and the smaller trade union grouping NACTU, which is in the black consciousness tradition. Their agreement of the need for unity presaged the very broad committees prepared to welcome a released Nelson Mandela.

Pretoria set great store on the municipal elections in October 1988 — yet over 90% of black people declined to vote (76% of those registered). When the ANC and Pan Africanist Congress (PAC) were proscribed in 1960, opposition was largely suppressed for more than a decade; today, the Government has been unable to hold down the level of popular mobilisation.

South Africa's neighbours

A very encouraging feature at the beginning of 1989 is the possibility of greater peace in the region. South African troops are already out of Angola, where they faced superior airpower, rising costs, and the risk of unacceptably high numbers of white casualties. More importantly still, Pretoria has agreed to the implementation of the United Nations plan for Namibian independence. It would be a dramatic move. Furthermore, President Chissano of Mozambique has met President Botha, and South Africa has promised again to assist Mozambique economically and not to succour the rebel MNR.

Past experience counsels caution. The South African Government has every interest, internationally, in being seen to be reasonable and to be negotiating. Pretoria first agreed to the UN plan for Namibian independence in 1978, and many times since has found reasons for delay. If independence does come, Namibia is even more vulnerable to disruption than Mozambique. It is economically dependent on South Africa, and Pretoria has formed and armed a number of regular and irregular forces which could be the basis for recruiting rebels after independence.

Pretoria has repeatedly pleaded its good faith in Mozambique, and denied supplying the MNR — only to be repeatedly shown to be lying, most recently by the US State Department. And if the South African army was restrained in attacks on neighbouring territories in late 1988, its surrogates certainly were not. The UNITA rebels remain very active in Angola. The General Secretary of the Council of Churches in Mozambique described 1988 as the worst year yet for rebel attacks, and after the meeting of Presidents, there has actually been an upsurge in MNR violence. The despatch from South Africa of non-lethal military equipment for the Mozambique army in November, however useful, can scarcely have reassured Mozambicans that Pretoria would rein in the MNR.

Nevertheless, the position is far more hopeful than two years ago, and it demonstrates that the South African Government does respond to pressure. The United States negotiators have clearly played an important role (with support from their counterparts in the Soviet Union). Britain's support of Mozambique and the Commonwealth countries of the Southern African Development Coordination Conference (SADCC) must also have been noticed in Pretoria. But most of these factors have been present at least since 1980. The major difference in 1989 is that South Africa now finds the financial burden of the war in Angola and Namibia very heavy. The immediate cost of the occupation of Namibia has been estimated between R500 million and several billion rands a year (compared with the total South African state budget of R53 billion). In addition Pretoria must hope that Namibian independence would lead the world to lift some of its sanctions and restore confidence in the South African economy. The South African economy is constrained by sanctions, making the cost of occupying Namibia a significant factor in government thinking.

Poverty
Through these events continues the system of apartheid which maintains wealth in the hands of the white minority. After the exhaustive Carnegie Inquiry into Poverty and Development in Southern Africa, Prof Francis Wilson and Dr Mamphela Ramphele conclude:

"The policies of separate development, anti-urbanisation, forced removals, Bantu education, the crushing of organisation, and, in more recent years, destabilisation, have been directly responsible for increasing poverty among millions of people. Indeed it is precisely this dimension of premeditation or deliberate policy in impoverishing people that makes poverty in South Africa different from that in so many other parts of the world."

Africans, who are more than 70% of the population, received in 1980 less than 30% of personal income. The process began with white seizure of 87% of the land, which was followed by the development of mines and industry under white control. In the apartheid model, black workers were needed on farms, mines, factories and white homes – but the remaining black people were relegated to overcrowded 'homelands' or 'bantustans'. A great migrant labour system arose, where breadwinners lived at their workplace and families in the bantustans. Between 1960 and 1982, the state compelled 3½ million people to move in pursuit of this ideal, and it continues to move them.

Land, wealth and income remain overwhelmingly in white hands

The system remains fundamentally intact today, for all the reforms. Land, wealth and income remain overwhelmingly in white hands. State expenditure on the education of a white child was in 1985/86 seven times the spending on a black child in 'white' South Africa and ten times the spending in 'homelands'. Nine million people in towns or on white farms risk eviction under the new amendment to the Prevention of Illegal Squatting Act. Legal restrictions on moving from bantustan to town have been eased – but those who want to move must have accommodation, and there is a desperate housing shortage in the towns: for example, almost half the households in Port Elizabeth's townships share accommodation. Those in towns face a bleak future: between 1970 and 1981, real wages rose, but the level of unemployment almost doubled (to 21% on one estimate). Since then, both wages and unemployment have worsened.

Meanwhile conditions in the bantustans reinforce poverty. There is too little land, far too few jobs, and a corrupt bureaucracy. It is no surprise that a 1987 survey showed exceptionally serious effects of malnutrition among rural children, and concluded that the position was likely to worsen in future.

With its mineral resources and its industrial base, South Africa ought to be able to meet the needs of its citizens. These assessments of increasing poverty for so many reinforce the call for an end to apartheid.

CHAPTER TWO

Current British Policy
– Pressure and Persuasion

Points in common

There is much in common between the long-term objective of the British Churches and the stated goal of the British Government. Sir Geoffrey Howe, the Foreign Secretary, has described apartheid as "neither Western, nor civilised, nor Christian". He argues that the changes made so far by Pretoria do not go anywhere near what is needed: a non-racial democracy with universal adult suffrage, in a country no longer fragmented into 'homelands'.

In accord with a very wide range of international opinion, the British Government states that a genuine national dialogue is essential, and that the most effective way to that dialogue is the route proposed by the Commonwealth Eminent Persons Group, which requires (i) a firm statement of intent from the South African Government to dismantle apartheid; (ii) the provision of freedom of assembly and debate, the release of all political prisoners, and the unbanning of political parties and organisations; and (iii) the removal of troops from the townships and the simultaneous suspension of violence by all sides.

In the wider region, the British Government supports the efforts of the nine countries of the Southern African Development Coordination Conference (SADCC) to reduce their economic and transport dependence on South Africa, including the rehabilitation of the key railway from Zimbabwe to the sea at Maputo. British support, including non-lethal military aid, has been much appreciated by the Government of Mozambique. When visiting the Maputo railway, which has been kept closed by the Mozambique National Resistance (MNR), in September 1988, Sir Geoffrey Howe urged Pretoria to respect the sovereignty of its neighbours and the inviolability of their frontiers. The Churches have called for greater aid to SADCC countries, noting that British bilateral aid is one third less in real terms than in 1979-81. But aid is now rising again, and the direction of British policy is welcome.

Broad agreement might also be expected on the criteria for assessing policy towards South Africa. Sir Geoffrey Howe has proposed that "at a minimum, policies (should) not make the situation worse". Sir Robin Renwick, the British Ambassador to South Africa, speaking to a South African audience, asked: "How can we seek best to overthrow apartheid without inflicting even greater misery on the people of South Africa, to say nothing of the neighbouring states?" These two propositions need to be clarified (a) by recognising that Britain can only contribute to the overthrow of apartheid, in support of South Africans' own efforts, (b) by recognising the general willingness of people to make sacrifices now to achieve gains in the future, and (c) by an assessment of risk and probability, since we cannot be sure of the consequences of a policy. The rest of this chapter considers how British Government policy matches up to these criteria.

Diplomacy

"The best form our help can take is pressure and persuasion, doing all we can to bring South Africans to start a genuine dialogue," Sir Geoffrey Howe has said. Britain makes representations to the South African Government both on the need for fundamental change, and on specific issues.

Yet diplomacy alone has clear limitations. In 1988, Pretoria did change its mind on hanging the Sharpeville Six, imposed

Britain has failed to build a clear understanding with the African National Congress

only a one month suspension on the respected *Weekly Mail* rather than the three months expected, and amended proposed restrictions on the flow of foreign aid funds to non-governmental organisations. These were important issues, on which foreign governments made representations. But though important, they were not fundamental issues, and, except in the case of the Sharpeville Six, the concessions were minor. It is also impossible to tell whether Pretoria responded to unalloyed diplomacy, or the threat of further sanctions (notably from the Federal Republic of Germany in the event of the Sharpeville Six being hanged), or indeed a bit of both.

Even within these constraints, British diplomacy has missed significant opportunities. A senior World Council of Churches delegation that met with Western governments in January 1989 commented: "Contrary to our experiences in Great Britain, the

Governments of the Federal Republic of Germany, France and the United States appreciated the urgency of the situation."

Britain has been sparing in vocal support of democratic leaders under attack by the Government. Most recently, when three UDF leaders and a church worker were convicted of high treason in December 1988, the United States commented on the grave implications of the judgment, and said: "We have been in constant contact with the defendants and know them to be men of goodwill working peacefully for a non-racial, democratic South Africa." Britain remained silent, pending the Appeal Court.

Britain has failed to build a clear understanding with the African National Congress (ANC), vacillating from cautious contact to Mrs Thatcher's condemnation. By contrast, the Commonwealth Eminent Persons Group and various church delegations have recognised the ANC's importance and shared its goals, even if disagreeing with some ANC policies. Other South African organisations working for an end to apartheid, notably the UDF, regard the British Government's role as unhelpful and often as on the side of Pretoria. This is a poor result for past British diplomacy, and a poor base for the future.

Signals
Britain has applied 15 sanctions, or restrictive measures, which are listed in Appendix A. Some of these measures, in particular the arms embargo, have a significant impact on South Africa. In each case, the decision was taken as a consequence of British membership of the Commonwealth, the European Community, or the United Nations, rather than on British initiative, and the Government opposes further sanctions. However, Sir Geoffrey does see the present restrictive measures as a signal: "to bring home to the South African Government the political message that change is urgently needed".

The British Government has promised to observe these restrictions scrupulously. Yet serious questions have been raised by the Anti-Apartheid Movement and others. There have been computer and radar sales which could be of use to the military. The voluntary ban on the promotion of tourism appears to have been carried out only through the despatch of two letters to tourist federations, and is not monitored by the Government. British Airways heavily advertises its South Africa flights, including a link to the USA which replaces the direct flights banned by the US Congress. Since the European ban on imports of certain categories of iron and steel, Britain has maintained imports – presumably legitimately – under contracts agreed before the announcement of the measures, or possibly between the announcement and the date they came into effect. Most marked has been Britain's encouragement of trade, which conflicts with its acceptance of the 1985 Commonwealth agreement that there should be no government funding for trade missions to South Africa.

With the exception of computers, these would not be violating the letter of the restrictions. But if scruples extend only to the letter, and not the spirit, the signal received in Pretoria is surely distorted. At the Commonwealth review of sanctions in October 1987, Britain refused to participate in a continuous evaluation and monitoring of the application of sanctions. The message brought home to the South African Government is not that change is urgently needed, but that Britain regards these measures lightly. And if the measures are taken lightly, what should Pretoria conclude about change?

Promotion of trade

The Minister of Trade has emphasised that Britain's restrictive measures are not intended to discourage legitimate trade with South Africa. British firms have to make their own decisions. Once they have decided, the Government's role is to support such companies and provide market intelligence through the British Overseas Trade Board. This support is carried out vigorously. The Chairman of the British Overseas Trade Board, Sir James Cleminson, said in October 1988:

"Looking back on the year there is a very clear message. That is that the UK has been a reliable – probably the most reliable – trading partner (of South Africa). . . . So, with the Government taking a helpful and positive stance, and a strong team of officials in UK posts in Johannesburg, Cape Town, Durban and Pretoria and in the UK-South Africa Trade Association (UKSATA) and the Department of Trade and Industry, there is plenty of support."

Numerous South African Government ministers, officials and business representatives have been received by the British Minister of Trade. Department of Trade and Industry (DTI) and UKSATA officials have given numerous seminars and presentations, including individual company presentations to directors and senior staff.

These efforts are having some success. After a dramatic fall in the wake of the 1985 crisis, the sterling value of British exports to South Africa rose 12% in 1987, and 18% (on an annual basis) in the first nine months of 1988.

By contrast, US exports remained static in 1987, at half their value before the imposition of sanctions (measured in IMF Special Drawing Rights [SDRs]). Japan and West Germany's trade grew even faster than Britain's. Yet in 1988, embarrassed

Apartheid is "neither western, nor civilised, nor Christian,"
Sir Geoffrey Howe.

by its emergence as South Africa's leading trading partner, the Japanese Government took a different line to Britain, leaning on companies to reduce trade: as a result, its 1988 trade with South Africa was 3½% below 1987.

Aid to black South Africans

Britain spent in 1988 £4½ million directly, and £3 million through the European Community, in assistance to black South Africans. The largest element was 500 scholarships at British universities, but Britain is also interested in the development of small businesses, and in community projects. The British Government sees the programme as a way of promoting

---

aid money empowers those who receive it, and weakens those who do not

---

internal forces for change in South Africa. The EEC has a rather different emphasis, calling its programme 'support for the victims of apartheid'. A future democratic country will certainly need the skills that are being imparted. The South African Council of Churches has welcomed the programme of positive funding measures, but is increasingly concerned that the British Government appears to see them as an alternative to sanctions.

It is clear to all that such positive measures will not end apartheid, and that is not their purpose. The relatively small size of the programmes inevitably means that they cannot have a major impact in, for example, promoting economic growth, or bringing about the emergence of a significant class of black entrepreneurs.

Furthermore, as the British programme grows and moves into areas such as upgrading squatter settlements and community-based primary health care, a warning has to be sounded if the programme is to meet Sir Geoffrey's minimum criterion of not doing any harm. A democratic South Africa will certainly need appropriate housing and health care systems if it is to meet the needs of the majority of the people but effective locally-based housing and primary health care schemes have to be based on the support of the community. At the moment, many local communities in South Africa are organised through civic associations and similar groups, often linked to the UDF. But these communities are also the principal target for the military's strategy of disrupting groups opposed to apartheid and replacing them with more pliant ones. Other things being equal, aid money empowers those who receive it and weakens those who do not; it is therefore crucial who gets it and on what terms it is given.

Nancy Durrell-McKenna

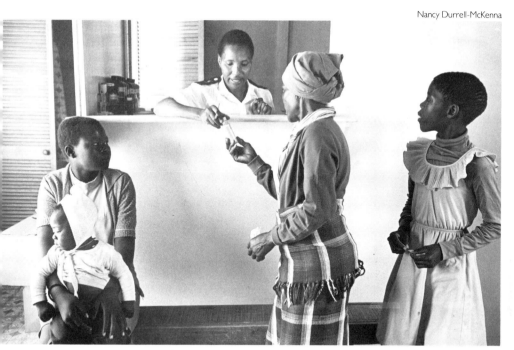

*A democratic South Africa will need appropriate housing
and health care systems to meet the needs of the majority
but, to be effective, such schemes have to be based on the
support of the community.*

The EEC met this difficulty by negotiating its programme with
South African Churches and an independent trust and agreeing
clear criteria for projects to be funded. For example, projects
should enjoy community support, and be run democratically.
Britain should follow a similar procedure.

The underlying logic of British policy

These various instruments of British policy, taken together, do
not constitute a powerful contribution to the overthrow of
apartheid, which was the aim suggested by Sir Robin Renwick.
Indeed, Sir Geoffrey Howe has emphasised that change will not
be rapid. But the British Government believes that change is
inevitable. In this view, the fundamental process at work is
economic growth, which will erode apartheid. British policies
are designed to assist the process. But how far does this logic
stand up? There are several arguments intertwined, which will
be considered in turn: the effect of population growth, the
effect on government of increasing resources, and the effect on
black people.

Population growth

On present trends, there will be eight times as many black people as white by the year 2000, compared with 4½ times in 1980. Sir Geoffrey concludes: "The means of life, and basic and social rights, cannot be provided for numbers like these within the straitjacket of apartheid." That is of course true. The South African Government itself has suggested that some eight million people, almost half the labour force, could be without full jobs in 2000 (assuming GDP growth at 3.1% pa — see article by Charles Meth, in *Orkin* 1989).

However, to state that the present system will meet the needs of the people is merely to repeat the core of the case against apartheid. One cannot assume that the Government will respond to the pressures of rising population by ending apartheid. Rather, current policy discussions on unemployment emphasise relief works, training, and a very expensive decentralisation programme to bring jobs to the 'homelands'. In Latin America such economic forces have not led to structural change, but instead to rising poverty, increased numbers of marginalised people, and tightened repression to protect the elite.

Resources and confidence for change

The British Government argues that economic growth will provide resources for black advancement, and create the confidence needed for political changes. This applies to South Africa the familiar argument that structural changes are very much easier in developing countries if the incomes of the poor can be raised without depressing the incomes of the rich, which is possible if the whole economy is growing. But the argument is irrelevant to South Africa unless the Government is in fact committed to attempt the necessary political changes — which it is not. Otherwise, increased resources can be used to fund repression, or limited reforms that distract attention from political issues. As the Executive Director of the South African Association of Chambers of Commerce has written, intending a different conclusion to be drawn: "Whatever a nation's goals . . . they can most easily be achieved by producing more resources through the growth of available output per head."

Likewise, government confidence from economic growth can induce complacency rather than change. It is noticeable that apartheid was tightened during the fast growth of the 1960s, while reforms were introduced at a time of ferment, rather than smooth growth, in the late 1970s and early 1980s.

Empowerment of blacks

The most serious arguments in favour of economic growth receiving the highest priority, concern not its effects on the Government but on black people. "Black economic empowerment is one of the keys to progress," President Reagan told Congress. The theory is first that economic growth leads to significant groups of blacks gaining economic power, and secondly that they can translate this economic power into political power.

Some of the arguments are rather clearly wishful thinking. Black-owned enterprise starts from such a tiny base (about 2% of South Africa's capital stock, and less of its GDP) that even dramatic growth rates would confer very little economic power on black business: economic ownership in South Africa is concentrated in the hands of a few very large companies. The small black business elite is readily incorporated into the

Unemployment and poverty are the common experience of life in the 'homelands'

present structure, rather than acting as a challenge. Likewise, even if the Government does make inroads on the huge housing shortage, a growth in the number of black home-owners is unlikely to bring political change. It is significant in this context that the National African Federated Chambers of Commerce (NAFCOC) is on record in favour of economic sanctions.

However, there are more significant processes. Expanding industries have required more skilled labour than whites could provide, and so jobs could no longer be reserved for whites; they needed more semi-skilled labour than temporary migrants could provide, so increasing the bargaining power of the existing workforce and facilitating the re-emergence of trade unions in the 1970s. Workers need education, and so spending on black education has had to be increased.

Improvements in income and welfare are of course to be welcomed. Yet, firstly, the beneficiaries of this process have been primarily urban workers, rather than the black community as a whole. A small black middle class grows, but the majority of the population are left far behind. Some benefits have trickled down from urban workers to relatives, and to hawkers, beer-brewers and other small traders. But, as noted earlier, families remain divided between town and 'homeland', so minimising the spread of income. Unemployment and poverty are the common experience of life in the 'homelands', and still people are forcibly moved there. Because of these conditions, people try to leave for the towns; but once they arrive, life as an urban squatter is also grim.

This concentration of the benefits of growth is likely to continue in the future, as new machines need fewer workers per unit of output: possible unemployment figures have been

There will be eight times as many black people as white by the year 2000. The South African Government expects nearly half the labour force will be without jobs by then.

30

cited already. It is an issue which concerns planners for a South Africa after apartheid, let alone a country with the millstone of apartheid still round its neck. Economic growth under the present structure yields very partial benefits.

Secondly, it is unclear how the British Government believes

Nancy Durrell-McKenna

this uneven process will be translated in future into political change — how 'economic empowerment' is translated into political power. The key problem, as Edward Mortimer pointed out in the *Financial Times* (29/3/88), is the nature of the change needed:

"The hope that economic growth will produce peaceful change is no longer much of a hope, since the change required is not in the socio-economic sphere but in that of political power — where the white community is much less likely to be swayed by economic argument until its own way of life is directly threatened."

Economic growth cannot be relied upon to empower the people to be able to win the necessary political change. As unemployment increases (even with economic growth), the bargaining power of trade unions would normally weaken. Above all, the process of empowerment requires more than economic improvements for individuals. The reforms won in the past came not simply from economic growth, but from a process of organisation among the people (and sometimes with additional external pressure). Internal organisation, and external pressure, will remain key issues, and it must be remembered that economic growth also builds up the power of the State to fight such organisation.

The British Government agrees that economic growth will not of itself guarantee the breakdown of apartheid. There are certainly examples of fast economic growth without political democratisation, for example in fascist states and the USSR under Stalin. It is hard to think of a precedent for the kind of political process which the British Government is hoping for in South Africa.

Political change as a precondition for economic growth
Whatever its virtues, the prospects for sustained economic growth at present are poor, certainly at the 5 or 6% a year necessary to absorb the flow of young people wanting work. The British Government accepts that a political change is first required. As Sir Geoffrey pointed out: "A clear commitment to ending apartheid, and solid progress towards that goal, are preconditions for investment and development." The British Ambassador was equally categorical: "If you want to have economic growth, you will have to discard the remaining features of the apartheid system. If you do not discard them, you will not have sustainable growth."

The fullest exposition has been given by the Prime Minister herself:

"Experience teaches us that you only achieve higher growth, only release enterprise, only spur people to greater effort, only obtain their full-hearted commitment to reform, when people have the dignity and enjoyment of personal and political liberty; when they have freedom of association, the right to form free and independent trade unions, and fulfilment of all the other obligations of the Helsinki Accords."

As the reference to the Helsinki Accords suggests, Mrs Thatcher was speaking in Poland, but the lesson is a general one and consistent with the British theme that a commitment to end apartheid is a **precondition** for growth in South Africa. Sir Geoffrey Howe himself has made the comparison between Poland and South Africa.

But if political changes are a precondition for adequate growth, the argument that economic growth will bring political change is rendered of secondary importance. Furthermore, it is central to the justification of present British policy that change is inevitable in the long run. But if there is a real possibility that Pretoria will not make the necessary concessions, why is political change inevitable, and how will it come about? There is a real chance, instead, of further escalation of violence and repression, great loss of life, and much destruction of the economy — exactly what British policy is trying to avert.

The crucial question then remains: why and how does the British Government expect Pretoria to make the necessary political concessions? There is nothing in the history of past relations with South Africa, or any parallel totalitarian state, to suggest that diplomacy alone will succeed on so central an issue as this.

Economic pressure

The other lever that the British Government has approved is economic pressure. But British approval extends almost exclusively to economic pressure operating through the market: "Economic pressures in South Africa which are the result of market judgments can and do have an effective political impact." As Mrs Thatcher explained:

"What really has happened is the ordinary people of the world saying: 'We will not invest our money in South Africa because of political instability. We do not believe the present regime can last. Therefore change will have to come about, and we would

FOLLOWING PAGES:
Many migrant workers from the homelands have to live in hostels near their work for 49 weeks of the year.

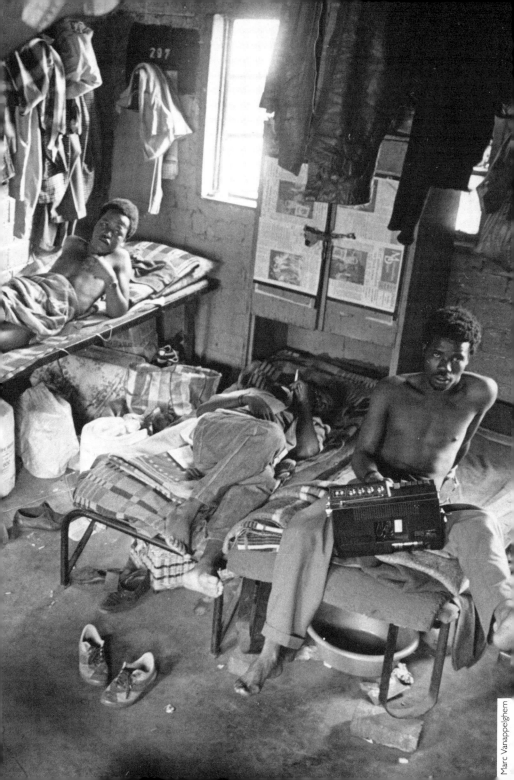

not risk extra investment there in South Africa,' and that has undoubtedly brought down the investment. . . . It is not so much government-to-government. This is the ordinary judgment of ordinary people and frankly, this is a much better way. . . . I believe it is that kind of individual and private institutional judgment that has far more effect than governments trying to influence things inside South Africa by government sanctions." (ITN inverview, October 17, 1987.)

Britain is the largest foreign investor in South Africa and South Africa's third largest trading partner

The political impact of these market pressures is presumably in raising the cost to the South African Government of pursuing its present policy, in much the same way as advocates of sanctions hope sanctions will operate.

But if Britain accepts that economic growth requires as a precondition a clear commitment to the end of apartheid, that Pretoria has not made that commitment, and that market pressures are politically effective, two conclusions seem to follow:

● **There are no grounds for the British Government to support the promotion of trade by those remaining companies who have decided a profit can be made.**

● **The British Government should look for ways of reinforcing these effective economic pressures. The great majority of Britain's European, North American and Commonwealth partners believe this can be done through further sanctions.**

Britain's continued acquiesence in these contradications at the heart of its policy invites the suspicion that policy is governed not by logic but by a narrow, short-term view of British interests.

British interests
Britain is the largest foreign investor in South Africa, and South Africa's third largest trading partner. This is an important economic stake, though it should not be exaggerated: it is less than 1% of British investment overseas and less than 2% of British trade. There are also several hundred thousand South African residents who are entitled to a British passport and to live in Britain. There is no case for putting the interests of British

'kith and kin' above those of the South African people as a whole. The British Government has instead suggested that it wishes to avoid them leaving South Africa for Britain.

In the short run, these interests might appear to be best served by the status quo – for example by trade promotion, especially if competitors were to hang back because of sanctions. In practice, however, the sluggish South African economy offers limited prospects now, and a very uncertain future. Firms with South African links are penalised in other countries, especially in the United States and within Africa. The negative image among black South Africans which Britain is gaining at present is not a good base for the future. This poor outlook is recognised by industry and few companies have joined the British trade visits to South Africa in recent years.

In a longer-term perspective, British interest in change is clear. Given its mineral wealth and industrial base, a democratic South Africa should be an economic success, requiring imports, probably offering investment opportunities, and providing a stimulus to the rest of southern Africa where British economic interests are also important. A long drawn out period of violence and stagnation could only harm British economic interests and increase the flight of British passport holders to Britain. A swift transition, minimising the levels of violence, would clearly be preferable to British interests (as to South African). The question remains how this transition could be achieved.

The risks of current British policy

The British Government accepts that its current policy is unspectacular, and that change by this route will take a long time. But the British Council of Churches' analysis of the current trends, confirmed by the urgent pleas of the South African churches, is that this route is unlikely to bring peaceful change. Economic growth is not enough, as the British Government recognises. A political initiative of the type proposed by the Commonwealth Eminent Persons Group is essential even to revive economic growth. Yet there is nothing in the British Government's policy, or its view of what is happening in South Africa, that would cause the South African Government to accept – and stick to – such an initiative. That gap is a very major weakness in British policy.

Instead, Pretoria is set on a course which, while incorporating some reforms, incorporates also a military strategy to destroy independent self-help community groups of the type both the Churches and the British Ambassador recognise are essential to genuine black empowerment. Pretoria's strategy is designed to head off the essential shift to a non-racial, representative government. The underlying purpose of the current reform strategy, as understood by the Churches, is that apartheid may survive. If this is not the understanding of the British Government, it would be most helpful if the Government

Change may be inevitable but the path ahead looks long and bloody

would explain its alternative view. For it seems that British policy, combined with these existing trends, is unlikely to contribute to that peaceful overthrow of apartheid that the Ambassador was looking for. Change may be inevitable, but the path ahead looks long and bloody.

What then of Sir Geoffrey Howe's minimum criterion that British policy should at least not make the situation worse? First, the current policy is doing harm to Britain's image among organisations working for democracy. Secondly, there is no doubt that the South African Government derives reassurance from Britain's policy – as Harry Oppenheimer, a prominent South African businessman, has said, South Africa sees Britain as providing protection. Indeed, given the divisions in the United States, and Mrs Thatcher's prominence and longevity on the world stage, Britain is seen as its most important protector. This may not be the signal the Foreign Office wish to send, but it is the one that is being received. The Commonwealth Eminent Persons Group said:

"If the South African Government comes to the conclusion that it would always remain protected (from effective economic measures), the process of change in South Africa is unlikely to increase in momentum, and the descent into violence would be accelerated. In these circumstances the cost in lives may have to be counted in millions."

If the South African Government was genuinely implementing the proposals of the Commonwealth Eminent Persons Group, it would be possible to argue that the South African Government needed to have its confidence boosted. Until that time, however, Britain would surely stand less risk of making the situation worse if it adopted a foreign policy stance more in line with the rest of the world community.

Current British policy must be judged against the alternatives. The BCC's grim analysis is that the situation in South Africa is likely to get worse than it is at present. If there is an alternative policy that stands a reasonable chance of promoting a less violent change, then Britain should take it.

CHAPTER THREE

Bringing Pretoria to Negotiate

Objectives

The BCC agrees with the British Government's stated overall aim that British policy should be to assist towards the end of apartheid, and the birth of a democratic, non-racial and united South Africa. The 'negotiating concept' put forward by the Commonwealth Eminent Persons Group is the most promising step towards that aim, in view of the wide support it has commanded. However, the BCC does not believe that present British policy is making a sufficiently effective contribution. Profound criticism has been directed at the British Government by church leaders within South Africa and most recently by the World Council of Churches Eminent Church Persons Group. A new policy is needed.

The first strand of a new policy should be **to offer clear support to the broad democratic movement in South Africa;**

The second goal of a new policy should be **to add to the pressures on the South African Government to open and continue genuine negotiations.**

A third goal towards the overall aim should be **to reduce the ability of the South African Government to suppress the black majority and to attack neighbouring states.**

A commitment to democracy

The pursuit of these goals requires Britain to adopt a different diplomatic stance, clearly aligned to majority opinion in South Africa. The 1986 British Council of Churches delegation to South Africa commented that the present position of the British Government, 'reflects much too clearly the views of the English-speaking business community with whom British business has close ties based on self-interest . . . (but which) politically constitutes a small minority whose motives are distrusted by urban blacks.'

Britain should associate itself more closely with the organisations working for democracy, including the UDF and COSATU. British ministers need to talk more often, and listen more often,

Marc Vanappelghem

A new British policy should ensure support for the broad democratic organisations in South Africa.

to the liberation movements. Britain should make more frequent representations to the South African Government, in the strongest possible terms, on such matters as the continuing State of Emergency, suppression of organisations, trials and bannings of leaders, and the closing of newspapers and other censorship. This kind of active diplomatic commitment to democracy arises naturally from Britain's own democratic

tradition, and is essential to establishing British credibility among South Africans.

Sanctions

Diplomacy alone is insufficient. The British Council of Churches believes that effective economic measures stand most chance of fulfilling the three goals set out above (see Appendix B), and the member churches of the BCC have individually and overwhelmingly taken the same view. Of course it is a matter for debate. There is nothing intrinsically moral about sanctions:

41

morality requires also that there be a reasonable chance they will work. The British Government is therefore right to insist on rational debate rather than slogans. But it does not help, either, for the British Ambassador to South Africa to accuse proponents of sanctions of 'moral necklacing'.

It is also important that these measures are not conceived as punitive, in the sense of being a punishment. They are intended to bring home to the South African Government the political message that genuine negotiations are urgently needed. But to bring home that message needs more than a signal of international displeasure. It requires measures that, taken with the internal pressure against apartheid, will convince Pretoria its existing strategy is not in white interests. As Malcolm Fraser, former Conservative Prime Minister of Australia and Commonwealth Eminent Persons Group member, put it:

"The purpose of sanctions would not be to destroy the South African economy. They would need to be constructed in such a way as to give the economy and the white population in particular a real body blow."

Support for sanctions

The British Churches take their lead, in adopting this position, from the South African Council of Churches (SACC). In 1985 the SACC National Conference called for disinvestment and economic pressure; in 1986 the SACC Executive adopted a call for comprehensive mandatory sanctions; in 1988 SACC focused specifically on measures against loans, arms, South African investment abroad, and other measures called for by the trade unions. In December 1988 the Anglican Church said: "We believe that the imposition of carefully selected and specifically targeted forms of pressure, including economic and diplomatic pressure, holds potential to bring about relatively rapid change."

sanctions are the last non-violent option open to us in South Africa at this time

The Roman Catholic bishops' position is: "We ourselves believe that economic pressure has been justifiably imposed to end apartheid. Moreover we believe that such pressure should continue and, if necessary, be intensified," so long as it keeps additional suffering to a minimum, and does not destroy the economy.

The Presiding Bishop of the Methodist Church, the Rev Stanley Mogoba, said in January 1989: "I regard sanctions as the last non-violent option open to us in South Africa at this time.... The question is no longer whether we want sanctions or not. The world has already made that decision. For me, the question is how to stop them. Scrap apartheid, and bring out a new South Africa: in this way, sanctions would become stone dead."

The SACC is reflecting a widely held view. Opinion poll evidence is somewhat confused, not least because it is illegal to promote sanctions. In an October 1987 poll, 67% of blacks believed that sanctions must be applied at least until the Government unbans political movements and abandons apartheid. In a March 1989 poll, 40% said other countries were right to impose sanctions unless South Africa agreed to get rid of apartheid, and 55% said they were wrong.

More significant than polls, however, is the unanimity across almost the entire range of representative organisations. The United Democratic Front, the ANC, the PAC, COSATU and NACTU have all called for comprehensive, mandatory sanctions. They are also in favour of at least some specific sanctions en route to that position. Their stand is the more remarkable because it is illegal; since early 1988 COSATU has even been specifically forbidden to debate it. There are small groups on the left opposed to sanctions, but the only organisation of any significance is Chief Buthelezi's Inkatha movement, which cannot be seen as representative of majority opinion among South Africans, despite its stronghold in KwaZulu.

Most Western countries have adopted stronger measures than Britain (the possible exceptions being West Germany and Japan, though in contrast to Britain, Japan is now trying to reduce its South African trade). In particular, the USA already has more restrictions, and a Bill banning all investment and trade (except strategic minerals) was approved in both Houses of Congress in 1988, though too late in the Congressional session to become law. The Commonwealth, too, with the exception of Britain, is unanimous.

The strategic effectiveness of sanctions

Some sanctions have a relatively direct effect on Pretoria's ability to suppress opposition. Despite the expensive development of a South African arms industry, the arms embargo has prevented the acquisition of advanced aircraft and other sophisticated weapons. This meant that South Africa lost its military superiority in Angola. Likewise computers are not just used in advanced industry, but also in weaponry and by the security services.

The economic effectiveness of sanctions

Most sanctions work more indirectly than the arms embargo, however. South Africa depends more heavily on international trade than other middle-income developing countries such as Brazil or Taiwan. Its exports are mainly raw materials – minerals and agricultural products. It does manufacture many of the consumer goods South Africans buy, but they are not competitive internationally. It depends heavily on the outside world for the machines and technology to run its industries, and for oil. Traditionally, it has relied on foreign capital to fuel its growth. In the future too, according to Anglo-American Corporation economists, some 10% of all investment would have to come from abroad if growth is to reach 3%.

As a result, there is general agreement that South Africa is vulnerable to sanctions, and indeed that the limited sanctions imposed to date have had an impact. As Mrs Thatcher observed, a major impact has been via the market. In 1986, the Governor of the Reserve Bank, Dr de Kock, pinpointed the negative effects of what he described as "financial 'sanctions' . . . (which) . . . have resulted not from conscious decisions of legislatures but from the deterioration over the period in overseas perceptions of South Africa's socio-political situation." This has been underlined in a detailed study for the Commonwealth undertaken by the governments of Australia, Canada and India. It has affected South Africa in two ways, and both have been reinforced by governmental sanctions.

Firstly, the lack of confidence overseas has been infectious, underlining the impact of domestic unrest. As foreign banks

South Africa depends heavily on the outside world for the machines and technology to run its industries.

refused to roll over loans and as foreign companies pulled out, South African firms stopped investing their money in South Africa, too. Total investment fell to very low levels – even less than was needed simply to replace old machinery (in 1984 gross domestic fixed investment was 27.5% of GDP, but by 1987 it had fallen to 20.4%). The President of the South African Foundation confirmed the link with government sanctions:

". . . there is no doubt that the (sanctions) package has had an adverse effect on domestic confidence. This lack of confidence is again and again emerging as the most important single factor inhibiting growth in this country."

Secondly, the refusal of banks to lend and foreign companies to invest means that little new capital is flowing into South Africa to balance the stream of dividends and repayments going out – about R20 billion net in the last three years, according to the Director-General of Finance. That can only be met by South Africa importing less than it exports. Imports were accordingly cut back heavily (by over a third in current dollars between 1980 and 1986). But imports are needed for growth, especially as South Africa depends so heavily on imports for capital goods. So as soon as the economy did start to grow again in 1987 and 1988, imports started spiralling, and when (combined with a sudden huge capital outflow) foreign exchange reserves fell to only six weeks' import cover, the Government had to damp down growth. It is now generally accepted that, **if maintained,** this will act as a permanent brake on the South African economy. In 1988 Governor de Kock reiterated his message:

"No one should under-estimate the harmful effects of these constraints. The need for long-term structural adjustment in the economy cannot be stressed enough."

Most in dispute is not whether sanctions hurt the economy – because they certainly do – but whether they have the desired political effect

Trade sanctions imposed by governments have reinforced this effect. Some imports have been more costly and for years South Africa has had to pay a premium to obtain oil to cir-cumvent the embargo, costing about $20 billion from 1979 to 1987, 80% above the normal market price. Export earnings have been cut. Exports to the USA almost halved from 1985 to

45

1987 (in dollars), though the total effect on South Africa was reduced by increased exports to other countries. About 15% (by volume) was exported in 1987, and South Africa had to cut prices to sell that much, so that coal earnings fell by a third, or $500 million. Steel and uranium exports are declining. "South Africa's export prospects have probably never been poorer," commented the Johannesburg *Financial Mail* in October 1988. There are ways around sanctions, but always at an extra cost to South Africa.

The political effectiveness of sanctions

Most in dispute is not whether sanctions hurt the economy — because they certainly do — but whether they have the desired political effect. It is very difficult to isolate the effects of sanctions from other influences, not least because almost everybody is agreed that the main levers for change are in the hands of internal opponents of apartheid. International sanctions are only one influence on a complex situation.

There are indications that the current limited sanctions have had some influence. Moves towards Namibian independence are, in part, the result of financial pressure both direct and indirect. At the very least, these moves disprove the contention that US sanctions ended Washington's influence on Pretoria. The most severe economic challenge was the 1985/86 negotiation with international bankers on terms for rescheduling debt. In this first negotiation (but not in the second) the bankers insisted on some moves to political reform; it was in this context (as part of the wider internal crisis) that the Government relaxed the pass laws and influx control, apparently giving bankers sight of proposals before they were announced.

The crisis of the mid-1980s certainly pulled South African business into more direct and specific advocacy of political reform than before, as evidenced for example in a high-level meeting with the exiled ANC in 1985, and a 1986 Business Charter produced by a widely representative group of business associations. This criticism waned in 1987, but there were signs of revival from mid-1988, for example in warnings from two of the most prominent business leaders, Anton Rupert and Harry Oppenheimer, that the proposed closer enforcement of the Group Areas Act would reinforce the pressures in the US Congress for tougher sanctions.

The imposition of sanctions by foreign governments had another political impact — as an indication to black South Africans of international support.

Nevertheless, it is clear that sanctions to date have not brought the Government to genuine negotiations. Opponents of sanctions claim this shows their ineffectiveness. Proponents argue

*The pressing need is to expose the futility of the present
South African Government strategy of repression with
reform.*

that the existing measures have not raised the costs of persisting
with apartheid high enough to bring the Government round.

Future prospects

What then are the chances of further sanctions having the
desired political effect? Historical precedent is much disputed,
but there are examples of success – recognising again that in
each case sanctions are only one influence among many. In
particular, sanctions against Rhodesia were an essential factor,
alongside recession and the war, in bringing Mr Smith to
Lancaster House (see Hanlon and Omond 1987, and Renwick
1981; for a counter view, Christopher Coker [in *Leadership*
1988/89]).

The pressing need is to expose the futility of the present
government strategy of repression-with-reform, and contribute
to undermining its viability. It is designed to eliminate effective
opposition and deflect attention from political demands by
some economic uplift in townships. If this is widely perceived

47

to be unlikely to succeed, there is a chance of the Government being forced to turn to alternatives.

Stronger sanctions stand a chance of undermining the repression/reform strategy in three ways. First, and least important, Pretoria will realise that the international community will not accept the strategy: it is a dead end as a way to ending isolation.

A stagnant economy will be less able to finance the repression/reform policy

Second, the economic strain of sanctions, by raising costs and limiting possibilities, continually holds back economy and government alike. A stagnant economy will be less able to finance the repression/reform policy, which is expensive. Police numbers have risen 50% since 1983 and will rise another 50% by 1994; acknowledged defence spending rose in real terms by 17% in 1987/88 and 6% in 1988/89, twice the increase in government spending overall. The policy also needs considerable sums for infrastructure: R34 billion has been projected for upgrading over the next 20 years, but this is clearly inadequate – seven million squatters need housing and services, and it is estimated that 400,000 houses are needed annually, let alone the costs of education and employment creation were they to be taken seriously. The experience of developing countries worldwide is that it is very costly to meet urban needs.

Third, sanctions increase business pressure on Pretoria. This matters (and certainly matters more than business leaders themselves admit) because politically the National Party (NP) is more aligned to business than in earlier years. In part this is for the negative reason that a section of the NP's old constituency, in the diehard white working class, have moved to the Conservative Party. But also NP policy gives an active role to business in such fields as training, and running privatised utilities. Utilities such as water and electricity are politically very sensitive, given the extraordinary tenacity with which township people have refused to pay service charges: business needs reassuring if it is to take them over.

In the last two years, there has been a degree of business acquiescence in the Government's strategy, structurally for example in the form of business liaison with the Joint Management Committees supervising military strategy at local level, and politically for example in the lack of concerted opposition to the Labour Relations Amendment Bill. This acquiescence was undoubtedly encouraged by the initial recovery of the economy after the 1985/86 debacle. As Archbishop Tutu put it: "Now the price of gold has gone up and the Government appears to have things under control, many business people . . . are no longer speaking in sharp terms about the Government changing its policies."

But sanctions, by consistently dampening economic revival and accentuating recession, send home a political message. The premature downswing of the economy in 1988 accordingly brought renewed business pressure for a political initiative. Business leaders certainly see the link to sanctions. Dr van Wyk, the managing director of the Trust Bank, told an audience in June:

"It has furthermore become imperative to achieve a break-through in the South African political logjam. A small, highly-traded economy cannot afford a prolonged trade and diplomatic war with its international trading partners. . . . An important step in this direction will be the achievement of a legitimate consensus between white and black leaders. A dramatic breakthrough is required in this respect and should certainly not be deemed impossible. The lasting benefits . . . are that South Africa could enter the 1990s without a State of Emergency, with white and black leaders forging the broad outline for a common destiny, with peace in the townships, lifting of sanctions, foreign capital returning, and the economy surging ahead."

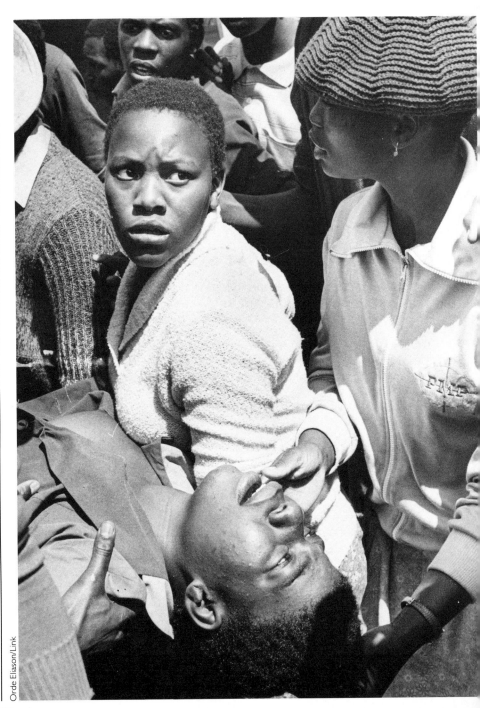

Orde Eliason/Link

CHAPTER FOUR

The Objections

A number of objections are often advanced against applying pressure on the South African Government.

Pretoria needs encouraging
It is argued that Pretoria is showing signs of movement, especially with regard to Namibia, and a tightening of sanctions will send the wrong signals. Timing the imposition of sanctions is of course important. Nevertheless, two points are fundamental. First, Pretoria shifted its position because of pressure, and it is important to maintain the pressure to prevent the evasion and backsliding that has characterised its stand on Namibia over the last ten years. Second, there is as yet no sign of a shift to genuine negotiations within South Africa: instead, repression has tightened.

Into the laager
It is argued that sanctions, by minimising the benign influence of the West, drive the South African Government back into isolation and apartheid, and widen the gap between liberals and conservatives. The Eminent Persons Group response was that the Government is already in isolation and committed to apartheid. For the West to maintain business as usual provides no pressure for change. In contrast, increased sanctions are the best chance of having a benign influence.

At present, the white monolith is cracking: a significant though small number of liberal whites have broken away; a larger group on the right – though without enough support to win a parliamentary majority – have left the Nationalist Party; the remaining Nationalists are uncertain of direction. This breaking of white unanimity gives hope for change; indeed it is inevitable if change is to come about. Sanctions certainly do not stop the divisions among whites; they may in fact promote division, by showing more clearly the costs of maintaining old-style apartheid.

LEFT:
Repression has tightened. A young woman was shot in the stomach by South African police after the funeral of three year-old Mitah Ngobeni also killed by police.

Destruction of the economy

Effective sanctions would inevitably damage the economy. (In the past, some critics argued that sanctions would on the contrary boost the economy, but recent experience, and awareness of South Africa's dependence on external technology, have discredited this view.) The extent of damage would depend on a number of factors, including how quickly the Government responded to the cost of present measures and the threat of future ones. But as the Anglican bishops pointed out in December 1988: "Official policy has created unjust economic structures which cause far more suffering than sanctions."

Future scenarios without effective sanctions are also likely to see a damaged economy, from both prolonged stagnation and a possibly long drawn-out, civil war. Sanctions would have the desired political effect long before the economy was destroyed, indeed studies of sanctions worldwide show that sanctions never go so far as to destroy economies. If there was serious damage, from whatever cause, recovery would be difficult; but there are precedents – not least Germany and Korea – and South Africa would be able to draw again on its mineral wealth.

Effective sanctions will hurt black South Africans

Effect on black South Africans

Effective sanctions will hurt black South Africans. There would be some compensating factors, such as a switch to more labour-intensive methods of production (because of a shortage of capital and imported machinery). And despite President Botha's September 1988 threat that sanctions will mean R9½ billion less spending on upliftment programmes for blacks over the next five years, such programmes are an integral part of present strategy and cannot easily be dropped. Direct military spending is not always the highest priority: withdrawal from Namibia, if it happens, would mean that the army in Namibia was thought less important than maintaining programmes in South Africa. It may be possible to target measures that particularly affect whites: one business estimate is that a third of the jobs lost would be white. But nevertheless, a sanctions programme working primarily through market forces cannot be finely targeted, and the general impact would undoubtedly rebound on blacks.

But major sanctions would hurt blacks less than the likely alternative of continued violence, economic decline and

Afrapix

As poverty in South Africa increased the South African Anglican bishops pointed out: "Official policy has created unjust structures which cause far more suffering than sanctions."

eventual disruption. Church leaders have pointed out that South Africans are prepared to accept increased short-term hardship, if the end of apartheid is hastened. And economic well-being in the short-term is in any case not the most important issue. The Rev Frank Chikane, General Secretary of SACC, has said:

"It is important to realise that for those who are victims of apartheid the debate whether the economy is going to be affected or not is not a priority. What is a priority is the child that has been killed yesterday or the child who has been brutalised in prison yesterday. . . . If your children are shot in the townships and you are working in a factory, the likelihood is that you leave the factory and go and take care of the dead child, because that issue becomes of priority, much more than the wages that you get because it doesn't help you to work for children who aren't there."

Sanctions will weaken the democratic movement
This is a most serious objection, and is advanced from across a range of the political spectrum – indeed one irony of the debate is the warmth with which the US State Department and the British Industry Committee on South Africa quote the Marxist Neville Alexander in opposition to total sanctions. The greatest concern is for trade unions, whose base may be weakened by economic recession. Unions may also encounter a more helpful reception from a foreign multi-national company than from a South African firm who buys the business when the foreign firm disinvests.

In response, three points. First, the trade unions have so far survived the economic crisis of the mid-1980s surprisingly well; but of course that is unlikely to continue indefinitely. Second, a great many trade unionists, above all in the mining industry, already work for a South African firm rather than a multinational. Third, granted this is a cost of sanctions, it has to be set against the potential benefits. But it does raise the importance, clearly recognised by the South African Churches, of listening very carefully to the union movement. That is not easy now that COSATU is expressly forbidden to discuss sanctions. But COSATU is clearly in support of comprehensive, and some specific, sanctions.

It is also suggested that community groups are damaged by the ending of social responsibility programmes when foreign firms disinvest. This is a real dislocation, but not so serious, if only because alternative sources of external funds (notably from Western governments and the EEC) have been growing rapidly at the same time. It also has to be said, though, that some of the social responsibility funding goes to groups making little contribution to the end of apartheid.

Sanctions hurt the neighbouring States
Even comprehensive sanctions against South Africa would not themselves have a dire effect on the neighbouring States, provided their routes to the sea were kept open and international arrangements were made for landlocked Lesotho. The real cost comes in Pretoria holding them hostage, not least by blocking those routes. South Africa's ruthlessness in impoverishing its neighbours would be tempered, because the

neighbouring States provide a market for $1½ billion-worth of South African exports and $350 million in railway revenue. But no doubt the damage would be real. Yet the Heads of State meeting of the nine Southern African Development Coordination Conference (SADCC) States have given their support to western sanctions despite the likely cost to themselves (this is different, though the British Government has not always recognised the distinction, from the immediate neighbours imposing sanctions themselves). As Simba Makoni, the Executive Secretary of the SADCC, put it in November 1987:

"Our countries are suffering enormous damage at the hands of the South African Government, both directly and by proxy.... Certainly we will suffer from the application of sanctions by the international community, but it is a cost we are willing to bear, in the conviction that the only alternative is to prolong our current agony for ever."

Sanctions would hurt the West
Dr Makoni went on in that speech to compare the small cost of sanctions to the West with the sacrifice in life, limb and liveli-hood made by the neighbouring States. The cost to the West of even comprehensive sanctions has often been much exag-gerated. The number of British jobs that might be lost is considerably smaller than the month to month variations in employment, and well within the leverage of the Government's macro-economic policies. In 1979 Britain lost exports to Iran worth two-thirds of exports to South Africa, without significant redundancies. Likewise, the West's dependence on South Africa for strategic minerals is not a major issue – only chrome and platinum are likely to cause any real difficulty, and that can be overcome. (On these issues, see *Moorsom* 1986, and on minerals *Hanlon & Omond* pp 243-259.)

Sanctions are unenforceable
An alternative argument is that sanctions would have no significant effect because they could be evaded. It is true that some sanctions are more easily enforced than others. Diamond sales would be hard to prevent, because small volumes of diamonds are easy to conceal and yet very valuable. On the other hand, coal or fruit have proved relatively easy to trace and so ban. Western computers and high technology have been successfully denied to the Soviet Union through an international licensing system known as COCOM. Oil imports could also be prevented (albeit with a small amount of evasion), given satellite surveillance and international publicity against

Major sanctions would hurt blacks less than the likely alternative of continued violence. Women of Crossroads call for protection from right-wing vigilantes and the right to rebuild their demolished homes.

defaulters. Sanctions have already proved to be enforceable.

Two factors tend to increase the effectiveness of sanctions. First, evading sanctions is costly: even if South Africa does manage to break a trade ban, its exports will fetch less and its imports cost more than at present. Secondly, and very importantly, the effect of even small sanctions is magnified by the market, as the 1986 financial crisis showed: business confidence falls, domestic investment dries up, and foreign banks and investors refuse to supply desperately needed foreign exchange.

Which sanctions are most appropriate?

If it is accepted that further economic measures could be effective, the question remains as to which measures. It is not possible in a paper of this length to enter into detail, but there are a number of careful studies of the potential of various different economic measures, and others are underway. (See particularly Commonwealth Foreign Ministers, *Hanlon* and *Omond, Orkin,* and *Riddell.*) From these studies, a few general principles emerge which command broad support.

Weight

First, the sanctions need to be a major threat, not a minor irritation. Pinpricks can be absorbed. This is why there is strong support for comprehensive sanctions, forbidding all economic ties with South Africa, imposed by the United Nations Security Council so that they are mandatory for the whole world. For example COSATU's 1987 resolution says:

"COSATU supports comprehensive and mandatory sanctions as the only sanctions which are likely to bring effective pressure which will assist in bringing about a non-violent, truly democratic and non-racial South Africa . . . COSATU believes that selective sanctions packages **as presently applied** will not be effective against capital or the State, (and) that they can cause serious regional unemployment . . . (emphasis added)."

---

sanctions need to be a major threat, not a minor irritation

There is much to be said for the international community preparing itself to go to the extent of comprehensive sanctions. Expert studies suggest that they could be adequately enforced, certainly at a cost but not a prohibitive cost.

Pending a United Nations decision on comprehensive sanctions, however, there are specific measures, which are more important than others, which command international support, and which could if necessary be steps on the road to comprehensive sanctions. Indeed, the COSATU resolution goes on to list some of them, including an end to loans and a stop to South African capital being invested abroad.

Interim measures of this kind carry more weight if they are part of a phased, graduated programme of sanctions. If Pretoria fails to respond to one phase of sanctions within a reasonable time, the next, tougher phase of sanctions would be introduced. The 1986 US Comprehensive Anti-Apartheid Act is drafted in this way.

Adherence to existing British measures: arms and trade

A first requirement for Britain to be taken seriously is enforcement of the existing sanctions, in spirit as well as to the letter. Trade promotion should be ended. The arms embargo should be rigorously enforced, and should clearly cover computers and other devices which could be used for military purposes.

Maintaining and reinforcing market pressures

In recent years, a very serious impact has been made through market pressures – the refusal of banks to lend and firms to invest. This is a view shared by the British Government. Taking measures to maintain and reinforce these pressures could therefore be seen as an extension of current British policy, rather than a repudiation of it. It is after all standard practice in general economic policy to influence the market, and appears to be what the Government is trying to do – albeit in the wrong direction – in supporting trade with South Africa. It is a particularly powerful approach because it magnifies the effect of a particular sanction: almost any set of measures would depress business confidence if South Africa believes they are meant seriously.

The most important measure is on **loans.** There are widespread calls for such action from within South Africa. The ecumenical Church delegation visiting Europe in May 1988 included an end to loans to South Africa in their minimum programme; in January 1989 Archbishop Tutu, Dr Allan Boesak and Frank Chikane called on US banks to demand immediate repayment of existing loans. Likewise COSATU put an end to loans and credits at the top of the specific measures in the 1987 resolution. Financial pressure is also the key area identified to date by the Commonwealth Committee of Foreign Ministers on Southern Africa who single out:

- **Restrictions on new lending and investment, including trade credits;**
- **a ban on insurance cover by official export credit agencies;**
- **tough rescheduling arrangements for existing loans.**

This is also an area where non-governmental pressure, from institutions and the general public, can have an effect. Campaigns for disinvestment have shown that banks and companies take note of public pressure in making their free market decisions. The key event is the negotiations between Pretoria and the banks (including Barclays, the National Westminster and Standard Chartered) on the repayment of US$11 billion of existing debt. The negotiations have to be completed by early 1990, and North American and European Churches are already making representations. Banks are being pressed to seek repayment of existing loans as rapidly as possible, and make no new loans.

Reinforcing market pressure has also been one of the main effects of **disinvestment** – international companies leaving South Africa. A large number of firms have withdrawn: 114 US companies left for political reasons between January 1986 and May 1988, for example. There are problems with disinvestment as practised so far: in particular, South African firms have been able to buy the factories cheaply, and foreign companies have often maintained important links after disinvesting. Nevertheless, disinvestment in the short run does depress business confidence (and absorb South African funds that might have otherwise gone to new productive investment); in the medium term, it denies South Africa both the latest technology and the crucial flow of new capital.

Trade
The US Congress will again during 1989 consider a full trade embargo. Measures short of that need to be considered keeping in mind COSATU's warning about the need for sufficient weight. The May 1988 Church delegation and Commonwealth foreign ministers gave priority to **coal**: existing bans, especially from France and Denmark, have had an effect and it is a major export (though Britain is not at present a major importer). Other vulnerable exports are **agricultural produce** (where Britain is the major importer, and Ireland has taken a lead in banning them), and **ferro-alloys.**

The crucial South African imports for a tightened embargo are **oil,** and **high technology.** The latter is a new area of considerable importance, which the US State Department agrees could be effectively embargoed using the legal and administrative machinery that prevents high technology flow to the Soviet Union. South Africa's major export by far, **gold,** has hitherto been regarded as hard to embargo. However, methods are being investigated, and this research should be pursued vigorously.

Undermining white confidence in apartheid
Both the Churches and COSATU have stressed measures that would undermine white confidence and standards of living, such as diplomatic isolation, a ban on direct flights, a more effective ban on tourism, and ending the recruitment of skilled personnel abroad. The sports boycott has shown that such measures can be effective, not least in 1988 discussions between rugby administrators and the ANC.

International monitoring of existing measures
Sanctions are inevitably more effective if there are mechanisms for monitoring and enforcing them. Existing monitoring

Sanctions can be evaded but coal and agricultural exports have proved relatively easy to trace.

systems are surprisingly few and in some cases reliant on non-governmental effort. The small Amsterdam-based Shipping Research Bureau, for example, has shown both the feasibility of monitoring oil shipments to South Africa and the effectiveness of publicity in deterring shipowners. Further investment in well-resourced and publicised monitoring would be a major help.

It is also important to minimise the extent to which third countries can undermine sanctions taken by most of the international community. There has been some success in international disapproval bringing both firms and countries into line, as illustrated by the Japanese Government's recent efforts to reduce trade, action in the Italian Parliament to reduce Italy's prominent coal and gold imports, and moves by Norwegian shipowners away from carrying oil to South Africa once their actions were revealed in the press. As well as Britain, Japan and

West Germany, attention needs to be given to Hong Kong, South Korea and Taiwan. Taiwan in particular has growing investment as well as trade links with South Africa, large foreign exchange reserves and an important computer industry.

This again is an area where both governments and non-governmental organisations can have an effect. For example, foreign companies and banks operating in the USA have had to review their South African operations because of the pressure of US public opinion. The United States Congress has given particular attention to ways of preventing other countries undermining US sanctions; proposed clauses to penalise the US operations of foreign companies active in South Africa were withdrawn after pressure from the EEC, but show what could be achieved.

The vulnerability of South Africa
Additional sanctions against South Africa are both feasible and desirable. Though the outcome cannot be certain, the chances of success are reasonable and the costs of doing nothing are certainly high. South Africa stands at the beginning of 1989 with its future economic growth precarious. Once more, there has been a huge outflow of foreign capital. There is little confidence among international bankers that South Africa will meet its debt

---

the economy is vulnerable, confidence easily punctured, and sanctions therefore more effective

---

repayments on schedule. Investment remains low, inflation rising, and the Rand, which fell 17% during 1988, is falling further. Gold traditionally rescued the South African economy, but the price is low and likely to remain low, and South Africa is now (on average) a high cost gold producer. The Standard Bank *Economic Review* in November 1988 hoped for a 'soft landing' but warned:

"Against the backdrop of the serious nature of the difficulties facing the South African economy, the major risk in most projections for next year is in the negative direction. If anything goes wrong, the slowdown may well turn out to be more severe than envisaged . . . businessmen should be aware of the risk and ensure they are adequately prepared. . . ."

In other words, the economy is vulnerable, confidence easily punctured, and sanctions therefore more effective.

CHAPTER FIVE

A Campaigning Church

The path ahead

The Church in South Africa for the most part believes the path ahead is hard, and set about with suffering. There is no sign that the Government is moving to end apartheid.

Yet the Church is full of hope – in its statements, and visibly in its township congregations. The Church universally is committed to turning hope into reality, "a pilgrim people, under mandate to search for the Kingdom of God", as the Anglican bishops of Southern Africa said in December 1988. In South Africa, most Churches see themselves having a special responsibility laid upon them, overall because of the sinfulness

---

The Church in South Africa believes the path ahead is hard, and set about with suffering

---

of apartheid, and immediately because most other organisations committed to democracy have been suppressed.

So the Churches of Southern Africa challenge the Government, and constantly seek effective ways to support the movement for change. On February 29, 1988, 25 church leaders, including the heads of the Anglican, Methodist, black Dutch Reformed, and United Congregational Churches and the Roman Catholic Archbishop of Cape Town, left the Anglican cathedral in Cape Town to march to parliament, carrying a petition. They did not reach parliament, because the procession was broken up by the police. The petition followed the silencing of the principal organisations opposed to apartheid. It read in part:

"Last week many of us issued a statement in which we addressed primarily the oppressed people of our land, for we

LEFT:
The end of a two-day conference attended by church leaders to discuss non-violent action against apartheid.

believe it is they who will decide in the final analysis when apartheid is going to be abolished. We urged them to intensify the struggle for justice and peace and we encouraged them not to lose hope, for victory against evil in this world is guaranteed by our Lord. . . .

"By imposing such drastic restrictions on organisations which have campaigned peacefully for the end of apartheid, you have removed nearly all effective means open to our people to work for true change by non-violent means. . . . Your actions indicate to us that those of you in government have decided that only violence will keep you in power; that you have chosen the 'military option' for our country. . . .

"We regard your restrictions not only as an attack on democratic activity in South Africa but as a blow directed at the heart of the Church's mission in South Africa. The activities which have been prohibited are central to the proclamation of the Gospel in our country, and we must make it clear that we will explore every possible avenue for continuing the activities which you have prohibited other bodies from undertaking."

The South African Churches have been suddenly thrust into extraordinary prominence by the suppression of other organisations. For the time being, the Churches can act openly, and so are asked to do so – for example in receiving released political prisoners. Above all, they can speak while others must be silent.

This vital significance of the Churches' voice is strengthened by its representativeness. Three-quarters of South Africa's 33 million people are Christians. 12 to 15 million are members of churches in the South African Council of Churches (SACC). There are of course divisions; not all of the black-led independent Churches, and few of the white-led and growing pentecostal Churches would support the high political profile of the SACC. But overall the crisis has been met with a remarkable unity.

Opposition to apartheid
The Churches accept the responsibility, because they believe that opposition to apartheid is central to the proclamation of the Gospel. With the exception of the white Dutch Reformed Churches, they spoke against apartheid from the start, for example closing church schools rather than introduce 'Bantu education'.

In the words of the Roman Catholic bishops in 1977, "Full citizen and human rights are necessary, on the grounds of the common humanity of all, taught by our Lord Jesus Christ". In recent years, as opposition to apartheid mounted in the country, the call in the Churches has become more central and more urgent. Church leaders called on voters to reject the 1983 Constitution of the Republic, the preamble to which claimed to be based on obedience to God. Reformed Churches worldwide formally declared the theological justification of apartheid to be heresy; opposition to it is therefore required of church members. By 1989 substantial groups of South African Christians, including the SACC and the SACBC, were debating whether the South Africa regime could be considered a legitimate government.

As the 1980s saw a flowering of open political movements in favour of democracy, the Churches became increasingly active in practical support. Some church leaders became patrons of these movements; some church buildings were made available as meeting places for striking workers. Individual church members became deeply involved, and suffered for it: from almost all of the 25 regional councils of churches, a staff member has been in detention. The then Secretary-General of the Catholic Bishops' Conference, Fr Mkhatshwa, was detained for over a year, and tortured in detention. The present General Secretary of the SACC, Frank Chikane, stood trial for treason; a staff member, Thom Manthata, was convicted.

Particularly as peaceful avenues were closed off, the question of whether the use of arms is justified became more pressing for the Churches. Church leaders call for justice, peace and an end to violence on both sides. Some are pacifist. Most Christians, in

The Churches believe that opposition to apartheid is central to the proclamation of the Gospel.

65

South Africa as elsewhere, are not: they accept that under certain circumstances, laid out in the theory of the just war, minimum levels of violence may be the route of least suffering. Rulers who persistently usurp the stewardship of God's authority must be removed, if possible peacefully and if not peacefully, then again following the principles of just war. In this context (and many ANC members are Christians), the ANC argues that it tried non-violent means alone for 50 years before taking up arms. Parallels can be drawn with other opposition to tyranny, for example with the French Resistance in the Second World War.

Standing for the truth

The response of the Churches themselves, however, has been to redouble their own efforts at non-violent action. As other organisations are silenced, church leaders believe they have a special responsibility, not just to speak out but to develop and implement non-violent strategies of change. Churches still have space to act that is denied to other organisations. In 1988 they launched the 'Standing for the Truth' campaign, recognising that it includes disobedience to unjust laws. One of their first acts was to support loudly and illegally the call for a boycott of municipal elections, because such elections offered no hope of genuine change.

In addition, the Churches have called for effective international pressure on the South African Government to force it to the negotiating table. The Churches of South Africa act very consciously as part of the Church worldwide. When the

---

Sanctions are not a panacea for all the problems of South Africa

---

Government threatened a Bill to restrict foreign funding, the SACC'S reply was theological – that the State has no right to divide the Body of Christ. Church leaders journey repeatedly to explain, to consult and to make joint decisions. As Frank Chikane put it:

"Faced with this crisis, coupled with the outlawing of almost all peaceful means of change for those who are victims of apartheid, **we as a Church in South Africa and the world over** felt that it is our Christian responsibility to intervene in this situation to facilitate change in a way that will cause the least pain and reduce the degree of violence and loss of life."

Afrapix

Police confront mourners at a funeral of eight people shot dead. Church leaders have called for an end to violence on both sides.

There is no illusion about the limits to international action. Sanctions are not a panacea for all the problems of South Africa. As the Anglican bishops said: "It would be wrong to suggest that reliance on international pressure alone will solve our problems. We therefore call for the exertion of pressure against apartheid both internally and externally."

British Churches have been concerned about racial injustice in South Africa for two hundred years. In the nineteenth century, the London Missionary Society made it its business to inform British congregations of conditions in South Africa, and to press the British Government to take action.

In recent years, the Catholic Bishops' Conferences in Britain and the members of the British Council of Churches have individually and together sent delegations to South Africa, issued statements, called on their own church people to take action, and made representations to the British Government. But the present situation in southern Africa demands that the case be set out anew, and requires an urgent response from the British Government.

CHAPTER SIX

The Modern Pharaoh

A South African reflection by the Rev Dr Francois Bill, Administrative Secretary, South African Council of Churches.

South Africa continues to be torn by crisis, by endless conflicts, trapped in irrational fears and plagued by senseless brutality. It is a country that is guilty of inhuman murders and deaths. A land, none-the-less, where the majority of the people yearn for human dignity and peaceful existence, and struggle at great cost to themselves for justice and freedom. A land whose majority are committed to full liberation from all forms of oppression. A land where the people are prepared to sacrifice even unto death for the establishment of a new society that will incorporate all the values of fundamental human rights.

Christian Aid/Elaine Duigenan

The Rev Dr Francois Bill, General Administrative Secretary, South African Council of Churches, addresses The Way Forward conference in February 1989.

And of course the cause of the dilemma, of the tragedy, of the suffering and of the death in South Africa is nothing else than apartheid. Apartheid has been declared a crime against humanity, one of the most hideous and heinous crimes in our modern-day world. An evil, a sin, a travesty of the Gospel. It's an illogical justification – a heresy.

The discussion is not about the nature of apartheid, and whether one can improve on apartheid, but the discussion, surely, is only about how we can attack this evil and eradicate it from the life of our society and from the life of our world. That cancer that is causing such suffering to countless numbers of people, and that cancer which remains a blemish on the conscience of all our churches for as long as we do not eradicate it.

Apartheid has been declared a crime against humanity

We, in South Africa, who are dedicated to eradicating this evil, and establishing an open, democratic, just and free society based on the principles of the Kingdom of God, are clear in our own minds that the way ahead is not an easy one, and that we will need to go on making sacrifices, and that we may even need to be prepared to die; as Archbishop Tutu has so often said, it may be necessary for more people to die before we finally reach the victory.

A costly commitment

You, in the United Kingdom, must decide for yourselves whether you are prepared to make a similar commitment and to express your solidarity and support for that struggle in our land. The commitment that is required of you is much more than just the offer of financial support, necessary though that may be, or of condemnatory statements against the excesses of the perpetrators of apartheid, important though those statements may be.

The commitment, which we ask of you, if you will, is one that will be costly. Because it will require you to make a sacrifice. It will require you to make a choice, and a choice that may well divide you in your own society.

The choice, you see, is not simply a choice for or against the present regime in South Africa. It is fundamentally a choice for truth and justice, for, or against, truth and justice, and therefore, ultimately, for, or against, God Himself. It's as basic as that, because we are dealing with an evil, a sin, something that is anti-God.

69

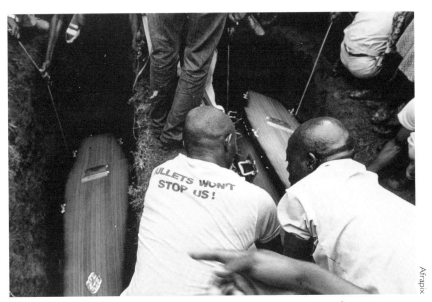

"A land where the people are prepared to sacrifice, even unto death, for the establishment of a new society that will incorporate all the values of fundamental human rights," the Rev Dr Francois Bill.

In order to understand the very basis of the choice which we are called upon to make, we, and you together with us, allow me, just very briefly, to refer to the biblical paradigm which we find in Exodus: Chapters 2, v 23 to 3 v 22. I think that there are, in these verses, some very important facts that we need to note.

Cry for help

The first one is that the oppressed people, the people of Israel in this case, had to make their cry heard. They had to express their agony. They had to cry out for help and assistance, and as the people of Israel groaned and cried out, God, remembering His covenant with His people, was concerned for them.

In the Republic of South Africa people have been suffering for more than three centuries. Suffering from the injustice of being oppressed, of being downtrodden, of having their land taken away from them and all that that means. And they have been making known their plight for decades. Decade upon decade.

Sadly this message of suffering, this cry of agony, is clearly expressed in the painful cries of the tortured prisoners in their cells, throughout the land; in the pains of the detainees who are driven to hunger strikes in order to make their plight known; in the death of prisoners, in the sobs of relatives as they bury their dead; in the protest of workers striking against oppressive and exploitative working conditions; in the resistance of people who refuse to be moved.

The cry is clear. The victims of apartheid are suffering and the question is: How concerned are you? Are you concerned enough to do all in your power, and in their interest? Yes, in your power, but in their interest, to end this inhuman, and cruel, and evil system?

Solidarity with the suffering

The second fact that we note in this paradigm is the concerned solidarity of the powerful God; the God of power expresses His solidarity with His suffering people in response to their cries, to their agony. He does so in a very tangible way. He makes it clear that He has seen how cruelly His people have been dealt with by Pharaoh.

He has heard their cries, He knows the extent of their suffering; to see, to hear, to know, to understand, is the basis for action. It is on this basis that God acts, and His action is very clear. He comes down to rescue them from their opponents,

---

The cry is clear. The victims of apartheid are suffering

---

from their oppressors, the Egyptians. That is the meaning of solidarity, to identify yourself with the people who are suffering, so that you act decisively and purposefully in order to bring an end to that suffering.

That means that you take your cue for action from the suffering people themselves. You act in your power, within the powers that you have, in their interest. Because, too often, we want to act, but we act in our own interest. God did not come down to set up negotiations between the people of Israel and Pharaoh, while they were still being oppressed. He did not come down to set up relief projects in order to alleviate the pain of the Israelites. He did not come down to promote positive measures and establish an ambulance service to take care of the victims of Pharaoh's oppression.

No, He came down to rescue them from their slave drivers; and what does that mean? To break the power of Pharaoh. To break the power of Pharaoh because it was only in breaking that power that they could be free.

So much of the concern and assistance which western countries in particular have shown and given to the victims of apartheid in South Africa fall into the category of conciliatory exercises, of alleviatory assistance, of ambulance service.

And while it is impossible not to come to the assistance of the victim, it is much more important to tackle the cause of that victimisation, by freeing the oppressed from the grip of their oppressors, and the only way that this can be done is by confrontation with the oppressor, with Pharaoh.

Pressure, in other words, must be placed on Pharaoh to such

"This message of suffering, this cry of agony is clearly expressed . . . in the sobs of relatives as they bury their dead," the Rev Dr Francois Bill

72

an extent that ultimately he is unable to continue holding the oppressed under his yoke. He's forced to let them go. There is no other way.

Agent of confrontation

The third thing that we notice is that God acts. But He acts through an agent, Moses. Moses is a reluctant agent. We can sympathise with Moses. He did not relish the task of having to

Afrapix

73

go and confront Pharaoh. After all there were very strong ties between Moses and Pharaoh. Pharaoh had brought him up in his palace; it was his daughter that had saved Moses from the bullrushes and from certain death, and because of these ties, these very narrow ties, it was very difficult for Moses, and so one understands when he says: "Who am I to go and speak? I can't go and speak to Pharaoh." And yet, go he must. And God assures him of the strength and courage that he will need to carry out his task, the task of liberating the people of Israel. The salvation for the people of Israel was liberation from the hands of Pharaoh.

In our present situation there can be no doubt in our minds that, despite all the historical, emotional, family, economic and

---

the United Kingdom is more on the side of Pretoria than it is on the side of the oppressed

---

political ties that exist between South Africa and the United Kingdom, the people of the United Kingdom are one of the agents who must confront the oppressors in South Africa.

The impression is clearly given that, while there may be a condemnation of Pharaoh, and of what Pharaoh is doing, it cannot be reformed. There is somehow an unwillingness to go the whole way and to exert the kind of pressures which will break the hold of Pretoria on the oppressed victims. And that is why the perception is that the United Kingdom is more on the side of Pretoria than it is on the side of the oppressed, despite all that is being done.

Now it seems clear to me that if the people of the United Kingdom, and particularly the Christians of your churches here, want to express meaningful solidarity with the victims of apartheid they need to respond to the agonising cries of the suffering masses in South Africa. You need to use your moral and political influence and put pressure on your own government to act decisively and unequivocally by putting the necessary pressures on the South African Government to do at least the following things: firstly, to lift the State of Emergency, and release all detainees and free all political prisoners; secondly, to allow the unconditional return of exiles, unban the liberation movements and allow free political expression; thirdly, to set a timetable for negotiations that will lead to a new constitution and the election of a new government; not an adaptation of the present, a new government which will be representative of all the peoples in South Africa in a unified state.

Ian Berry/Magnum

"... to see, to hear, to know, to understand, is the basis for action," the Rev Dr Francois Bill.

Pharaoh under pressure

It should be abundantly clear to those who truly desire to come to the assistance of the victims of apartheid, that we are dealing here with a modern-day Pharaoh that is as stubborn, if not more stubborn, than the Pharaoh of old. And just as that old Pharaoh was placed under pressure, repeatedly – I underline the word repeatedly – through plagues so, too, the apartheid Pharaoh needs to be put under pressure, continuously and repeatedly, because otherwise he will not let the slaves go free. That is why it is so important for the United Kingdom to respond to the call of the people for meaningful and purposeful pressures that will force Pretoria to the negotiating table.

To do so, as so many people believe, is not to destroy the chances of conciliation between the various sectors of our population. On the contrary, it is to ensure that before it is too late the best chances of that conciliation take place. But it is also to ensure that they take place, on the basis of apartheid having been eradicated, on the basis that wrongs have first of all been redressed, that justice is first of all done, that human dignity is first of all restored.

The Response

CHAPTER SEVEN

Dialogue and Steady Pressure – The Best Way

The Rt Hon Lynda Chalker, MP, Minister of State at the Foreign and Commonwealth Office:
I welcome the opportunity to explain British Government policy on southern Africa, at a time when significant developments are taking place in that part of the world. I have read your description of British policy. I can only say, with some regret, that I find it, in places, rather distorted. But I do say that I find it both timely and highly necessary to set the record straight. Because I, too, believe there must be dialogue, and not just dialogue between us here, but dialogue between black and white, government and non-government in South Africa.

the Government are very much aware of the valuable work done by the Churches in South Africa

Now let me begin by saying that the Government are very much aware of the valuable work done by the Churches in South Africa. I was lucky enough to see a little of this for myself last November when I attended a service in the main Anglican Church in Soweto.

The voice of the Church has become increasingly influential in an area where so many other forms of peaceful extra-parliamentary dissent have been stifled.

We try to keep ourselves abreast of Church thinking in South Africa by maintaining regular contact with church leaders, black and white, not only there, but in the UK too. And many of

Rt Hon Lynda Chalker, MP, Minister of State at the Foreign and Commonwealth Office, addresses The Way Forward conference at Church House, Westminster

LEFT:
"The voice of the Church has become increasingly influential in an area where so many other forms of peaceful extra-parliamentary dissent have been stifled," Rt Hon Lynda Chalker.

79

you will know that more recently, Sir Geoffrey Howe had a long meeting with a group of Eminent Church Persons established by the World Council of Churches. Of course they did not agree on all points. But, as Sir Geoffrey told the House of Commons on February 8, he listened attentively for an hour and a quarter and with respect to what the delegation had to say.

We are always ready to listen. But may I just ask that in return others please listen to our views and our arguments too. For just as we in Government consider it vitally important to keep lines of communication open, so it must be essential for the Churches' views to be formulated on the basis of the fullest possible information and of reasoned argument.

Abolition of apartheid

I hope I do not need to remind you of the fundamental objective of our policy towards South Africa because it is precisely the same as your own. We seek, and we will continue to press for, the total abolition of apartheid and its replacement through peaceful means by a non-racial representative system of government acceptable to all the people of South Africa. And like you, we want that change to come as soon as possible.

And as the Prime Minister recently and forcefully told the editor of the leading Afrikaans newspaper *Beeld:* "Apartheid is contrary to my whole philosophy, which is that people should be able to live where they like in their own country, exercise their full democratic rights and advance according to merit, not the colour of their skin."

Like you, we are deeply disappointed, in fact infuriated, I might almost say, at the lack of progress towards fundamental change in South Africa. We continue to urge the South African Government to take all the steps for which the international community has been calling: and first among these should be the immediate and unconditional release of Nelson Mandela and all other political prisoners and detainees.

But like you, the British Government remain extremely concerned at the number of people still held without charge (let alone trial) in South Africa. It is indefensible that some people have now been held in prison without charge for more than two years. We have put our views forcibly to the South African Government on many occasions. Yes, indeed, we do make these representations weekly, even sometimes daily, on behalf of detainees, of that you need have no doubt.

That is why there was some encouragement when we had an undertaking given by the South African Minister for Law and Order to carry out an urgent review of all detainees' cases. We welcome the releases that have been made. We trust they will be the first of many, and that the many will follow soon.

We also continue to press for the unbanning of the African National Congress and other political organisations too, and the rescinding, the total rescinding, of the State of Emergency. This would give evidence of a willingness to engage in a genuine national dialogue with credible black South African leaders. We hope it will come.

Steady pressure

But you know it would be an illusion to believe that external powers can somehow decide the future of South Africa. The solution to South Africa's problems must be found by South Africans themselves, black and white. We have made clear repeatedly that what we seek is a non-racial, representative system of government. It is not for outsiders to lay down detailed prescriptions.

That is why our policy is one of steady pressure. We encourage where we can. We seek to persuade those who hold power that change is indeed inevitable, and that to start negotiations for fundamental change is in their own interest.

Just as important, on a day-to-day basis we are engaged in helping the victims of apartheid: both those who suffer its economic injustices and those whose human rights are abused through detention without charge; forced removals; and all the repressive machinery of the State of South Africa.

The results

It may surprise some of you, but I have to say – our policies have produced results. Not as many as we want, but they have produced results. The last few months have seen the release of some well-known political prisoners such as Zephania Mothopeng and Harry Gwala; the freeing from detention of Zwelakhe Sisulu and other detainees; and the reprieve, thank God, of the Sharpeville Six. On the legislative front we have seen

---

We want to see all detainees released, freedom for all political prisoners and an end to the stifling of free expression

---

liberalising amendments adopted to the Group Areas Act. The South African Minister for Constitutional Development has announced that proposed harsh enforcement provisions of that Act would be dropped.

And all those issues have been the subject of frequent representations by Her Majesty's Government.

But, I am nevertheless the first to agree that much more, so much more, is needed. We want to see all detainees released, freedom for all political prisoners, including of course Nelson Mandela; and an end to the stifling of free expression. That's why we were disappointed to find that two more publications have recently been banned for three months.

But more fundamentally, we want to see the Group Areas Act, the Population Registration Act, and other primary apartheid legislation, not amended, not reformed but abolished totally, and please never forget that.

So, here is my answer to a call made in *The Way Forward.* I can assure you that we shall continue to press the South African Government to act on these basic issues, as well as making representations, as often as may be necessary, whether it be against repression or the frequent abuses of human rights. I would only add the caution that such representations are often more effectively made when they are made privately, not shouted from the rooftops. It's the results we look for, not the publicity.

Violence

Now, I think there is a growing recognition, certainly amongst many of the people that I've spoken to in South Africa, and I'm talking about black people in South Africa, that fundamental change is going to be a long haul. Of course we understand the frustration and the impatience of those who have suffered injustice for so long, far too long. But I must stress a very deep and sincere belief that violence is no solution. Violence is not only wrong, it delays the process of change by polarising opinion, and by further alienating the white community which has to be persuaded of the need for change. That is why we condemn the use of violence from whatever quarter.

Sanctions

And then there are those too who have looked at sanctions as the 'quick fix' to the problems of South Africa.

I ask where is the evidence that sanctions have worked in the past to bring about peaceful and positive political change? Yes, limited restrictive measures have been agreed and enforced by the European Community. The United States has gone further. But to what effect? Did Congressional sanctions stop the South African Government from banning 17 extra-parliamentary opposition groups just one year ago?

Let me quote from the US President's Report to Congress in 1988 on the Comprehensive Anti-Apartheid Act of 1986. And he said this: "The Act has reduced US leverage, hardened the South African Government's determination to resist outside

Afrapix

"The British Government continues to press for the unbanning of the ANC, other political organisations and the total rescinding of the State of Emergency," Rt Hon Lynda Chalker.

pressure, and increased the appeal of ultra-conservative movements."

I have to say that we agree with that.

Punitive sanctions would destroy what leverage we have with the South African Government. And worse, they would harm the very people we wish to help

---

The effect of sanctions

Let there be no doubt: undermining the South African economy tempting as it may be, to some, would hit black South Africans first and hardest. Certainly white South African living standards would be hit. By what? 10, 20, even 50%? But what about the black thrown out of work? His livelihood is affected 100%. What is to become of his family?

The recent Carnegie Report on poverty in South Africa paints a shocking picture. It is very much to the discredit of the South African Government. But are we to make the problem worse? The answer in our case is no.

And nor would sanctions only hit South Africa. The Front-Line States, linked as they are to the South African economy, would suffer severely.

Britain is investing willingly, and heavily, in aid to these countries, with the objective of reducing their dependence on South Africa. We are not willing to sabotage our own efforts.

So let us look for a moment; what are those most immediately affected saying? We heard with interest, a change in tone from some voices within South Africa itself, including the Churches there. I have to say I am disappointed that *The Way Forward* dismisses these so lightly.

I recognise, and share, the deep emotions which apartheid arouses. I share them absolutely. But I also accept the good faith of those who espouse sanctions. It does no service to their cause to ignore their views or to omit views, evidence or arguments when they run in the opposite direction.

If I may, I want to speak of Aggrey Klaaste, whom I met in November, the much-respected editor of the *Sowetan*. He has written: "Most blacks oppose sanctions because they know they will lead to more black unemployment." I've discussed that with him. I know that is not only sincerely meant, it is well founded.

Church statements

Concerning quotes from recent statements by the South African Anglican and Catholic bishops, may I say, I too have studied those statements with much interest. I have read them in full. As you record, the Catholic bishops' support for economic pressure was conditional upon keeping additional suffering to a minimum and not destroying the economy.

I would recall that the Commission established by the Catholic Bishops' Conference to look into the issue, reported that sanctions have, and I quote: "considerable negative effects". But just as significant the Anglican bishops' statement which you quote in part, also called for, and I quote again: "forms of action which avoid, as far as possible, further unemployment".

If I may be blunt for a moment: you cannot have it both ways. Economic sanctions are destructive. There are none which "avoid unemployment" or "keep additional suffering to a minimum" or "do not destroy the economy".

Restrictive measures

And while on the subject of selective or misleading quotations, let me take issue with the description of our performance on the restrictive measures we have agreed to implement and do implement. *The Way Forward* speaks of 'serious questions' being raised over our claim scrupulously to implement our international undertakings. To take just one example of how this issue is treated, a US State Department report is cited in terms which may have led some of you to conclude that the

Government had been lax in our observation of the mandatory UN Arms Embargo.

Well, for whatever reason, *The Way Forward* omits one key phrase from the State Department report: "The British Government has diligently enforced the UN Arms Embargo." And nor does your paper acknowledge that offenders have been fined heavily and in some cases sent to prison. That has happened. If others offend in future it will continue to happen.[*]

So that is why, it is against this background I was sorry to see a programme centred on further economic sanctions.

I sincerely believe that would be entirely counter-productive. There is no easy solution. We must and will persist with our policy of working patiently, yet persistently, towards dialogue; of bridge-building; of construction rather than destruction; of steady pressure. I believe this offers the best way forward towards peaceful but fundamental change.

Positive measures

That is why we are engaged in practical positive measures on the ground to help black South Africans. We see our programme of aid to black South Africans as one important way of promoting the internal forces for change in South Africa.

Since 1979 we have been offering training for a future in which all South Africans will have their rightful share and our programme is rapidly expanding. We are in the middle of a five year programme in which we expect to spend over £25 million in direct bilateral aid; on scholarships for blacks in Britain and in South Africa, and on a range of other education and social projects. This current year we are sponsoring 500 students. This number will rise to 650 by the end of the year and to 1,000 by the end of 1991.

In addition to that we are contributing some £3 million annually to the European Community's aid budget for black South Africans, and substantial further sums to the United Nations and Commonwealth scholarships schemes.

We are also pressing ahead with programmes of economic and security assistance to the neighbouring states. And these are substantial. They help the efforts of the Southern African Development Conference to reduce the economic and transport dependence of these states on South Africa. Since SADCC was formed the United Kingdom has contributed:
– over one thousand million in bilateral aid to the SADCC states;

---

[*]In the light of this criticism, the sentence to which Mrs Chalker refers has been removed from the main text. It originally read: "In 1987 the US State Department reported that Britain was one of seven countries involved in the supply of military equipment to South Africa."

— £60 million in pledges to SADCC projects (mostly in the vital transport sector)
— Approximately £104 million through the European Community to SADCC and its members over the current four year period up to 1990, plus one fifth of the cost of European Community food aid to the region as a whole.

A false picture

Let me conclude by returning to the point at which I started: the basis of our policy is our profound detestation of racial discrimination. Too often the policy of Her Majesty's Government is characterised as 'opposition to sanctions: therefore pro-apartheid'. I trust it is now clear, if it was not at the outset, that this is a totally false picture.

Britain is engaged in South Africa at all levels and with all sides. We cannot be otherwise if we hope to seek to influence those in power in that country: as my colleague, Simon Glenarthur recently told the House of Lords, and as I am sure I do not need to tell this gathering, you do not convert a country to Christianity by withdrawing the missionaries.

We shall continue to be engaged until the unjust system of apartheid is totally dismantled, step by step. Change in South Africa is inevitable. It will happen. Our role, and that of the Churches outside and within South Africa, should be to encourage the forces for change to make the transition as smooth, as peaceful and above all as speedy as possible.

CHAPTER EIGHT

With One Voice

The Rt Rev Simon Barrington-Ward, Bishop of Coventry and Chairman of the International Development Affairs Committee of the Board for Social Responsibility of the General Synod of the Church of England.

At the end of a book such as this, we need to get back to the very roots of the matter, to keep faith with those leaders marching to the South African Parliament in 1988. They are the representatives of the real voice we should be hearing. So many faces rise up before us today: the faces of those who have suffered within South Africa itself, the faces of those who many of us have met in the refugee camps on the edge of Mozambique. An overwhelming number of them cry out to us: "What are you doing? How can you help us?" The Catholic and Anglican bishops, COSATU and the UDF, stifled in many ways but still able to speak, are all talking with that one voice.

The Rt Rev Simon Barrington-Ward, Bishop of Coventry, at The Way Forward conference

I am saddened that others are seeking at the present time to point to other, so-called more moderate, voices in South Africa, as if the deepest moderation and magnanimity were not open to us through the very people of whom I am speaking.

There is a generation of leadership now in South Africa, many of whom are silenced and weakened by imprisonment

---

I am reminded of the situation shortly before Rhodesia became Zimbabwe, when all sorts of enlightened voices of business and the British Government were pointing to people whom they said were the real leaders, and the British Council of Churches was pointing unequivocally to Mugabe and Nkomo. When the time came, the rest dropped away like a wraith, like a mist, like a nonsense.

There is a generation of leadership now in South Africa, many of whom are silenced and weakened by imprisonment, kept

away from the opportunities that they could have to control and direct opinion. If they were released, we could see a moderate and unified opinion across the whole country. We must grasp their hands. If we are not prepared to link with those who at present have a concern for a whole, integrated, harmonious South Africa, then we shall find a generation emerging who are more deeply embittered.

The deterrent effect

Attempts are made to suggest that the voice we hear, with its inexorable call for much deeper action, is not representative. There is a desperate effort going on somehow to deflect us with talk of quotations being snatched from here and there. I do not believe we have distorted the Catholic bishops' position: the document quoted by Mrs Chalker was a report to the Bishops' Conference (not by the Bishops' Conference). After discussion the President of the Conference reaffirmed the position that we have quoted.

Neither is the Anglican bishops' call for economic pressure invalidated by their wish to avoid unemployment 'as far as is possible'. It makes a great deal of sense to adopt those sanctions that are likely to have the necessary effect on the South African Government with as little hardship and suffering as possible.

I personally question the argument concerning black suffering. Long before that we will see white people feeling the pinch, and then the threat of further sanctions will have a deterrent effect. As these initiatives begin to roll the very pressure of the deterrent will do a great deal to shift white opinion.

A recent opinion poll has suggested that the proportion of black South Africans in favour of international sanctions has fallen to 40%. Yet 40% is high support for a position which cannot legally be advocated. Free debate is impossible. We must press the more vigorously for freedom of expression and the unshackling of political organisations. In the meanwhile, sadly, opinion polls tell us little.

We welcome the opportunity for the continuing dialogue to which Mrs Chalker refers. She is someone who is willing to entertain that dialogue, and has helped us to speak – and argue – with her. We shall continue to do so. We have certainly no wish to give a distorted picture of government policy. In this book, we have corrected the one instance she cited.

Yet her speech underlined once more the limits within

LEFT:
"So many faces rise up before us today: the faces of those who have suffered within South Africa," the Rt Rev Simon Barrington-Ward.

*"If we are not prepared to link with those who have a
concern for a whole, harmonious South Africa . . . we shall*

Afrapix

*find a generation who are more deeply embittered," the Rt
Rev Simon Barrington-Ward.*

91

which the British Government operates, the reliance on inevitable change and the long haul which to us is implausible. And can it really be argued that the leverage of the United States was reduced by its 1986 sanctions package, in the light of the subsequent Angola/Namibia settlement and Pretoria's current pressure for a similar negotiation led by the United States over Mozambique?

The crucial moment
The time is short. As Francois Bill emphasised, a timetable is needed. South African Christians have stressed the theological

---

if this opportunity is missed, the loss for the Church, for the Gospel and for all the people of South Africa will be immeasurable

---

significance of this moment of history. "For many Christians in South Africa, this is the kairos, the crucial moment, the moment of grace and opportunity, the favourable time when God issues a challenge to decisive action. It is a dangerous time because, if this opportunity is missed and allowed to pass by, the loss for the Church, for the Gospel and for all the people of South Africa will be immeasurable. Jesus wept over Jerusalem. He wept over the tragedy of the destruction of the city and the massacre of the people that was imminent, 'and all because you did not recognise your opportunity (kairos) when God offered it'" – from The Kairos Document: *Challenge to the Church.*

This is a kairos indeed, a crucial moment, and it must not be evaded. "If you had known, in this key moment, this your day, the things that belong to your peace"; these are the words that must be addressed to Britain at this time.

There are new opportunities for international intervention in one of the great tragedies of our world. The Namibia settlement has shown that change is possible. The Soviet Union's immovability on southern Africa has cracked. The ANC has reaffirmed its preference for a negotiated resolution to the conflict, provided that there is a clear commitment to creating a democratic, non-racial and united South Africa, a commitment demonstrated by practical deeds. The reception given to Mrs Thatcher when she visited the front line states shows that Britain has an important role to play.

The paths ahead
Opportunities have to be seized, or the moment will pass. The South African Government has two paths before it. One path is

Marc Vanappelghem

"This is our own moment of truth ," the Rt Rev Simon Barrington-Ward.

marked in 1989 by continued detentions by the Prevention of Illegal Squatting Act, by the Foreign Funding Act which threatens the Churches, and by the 24% increase in defence spending, despite the Angola/Namibia settlement.

How can Pretoria be turned from this path to the path of genuine negotiation? I do not believe that persuasion alone will be enough, any more than it was in Namibia.

Twice in her presentation, Mrs Chalker spoke of the need for 'steady pressure'. The most effective pressure now would be some kind of really sharp action from international governments and business together. Most recently, the April 1989 Synod of Bishops of the Anglican Church of the Province of South Africa, singled out the need for pressure on air links and on bank loans to South Africa. That is what is set out in the Call to Action – action on trade, on air links, and on loans. That is what is needed to convince Pretoria that its interests do not lie in continuing down the present road of repression.

By all means Britain must stimulate a dialogue. But it must be combined with sufficient pressure to ensure that the dialogue succeeds. With one voice the true leaders of the South African people are asking us to support this approach. This is our own moment of truth. We must now respond with one voice, and with one clear programme of action.

CHAPTER NINE

A Call to Action

Britain's responsibility

Britain has a special responsibility in southern Africa, where for two centuries it was the main imperial power. It could now play a greater part in bringing about change.

The British Government is already committed to do what it can to contribute to the ending of apartheid and the establishment of a democratic, non-racial and united South Africa. Yet this commitment is widely questioned in South Africa by both black and white. They see instead a Britain shielding Pretoria from international pressure, and deeply suspicious of the organisations pressing for democracy and enjoying widespread popular support.

● **The British Government should offer clear support to the broad democratic movement in South Africa, in particular by more public protest about the trials, detentions, bannings and assassinations of its leaders.**

The immediate aim of a genuine national dialogue, along the lines proposed by the Commonwealth Eminent Persons Group and based on a commitment to end apartheid and introduce democracy, is shared by the African National Congress and the international community including Britain. Yet a method must be found for convincing the South African Government to open such negotiations and to remain committed to them. Economic growth would not do so, and in any event the British Government believes that a political initiative to end apartheid is a pre-condition for sustained economic growth.

● **Britain should stop sending counter-signals. In particular Britain should cease promoting trade with South Africa.**

The British Government believes that economic pressures, through the market, can be effective in influencing the South African Government. The Commonwealth and the Churches have emphasised the importance of financial decisions. So:

●**British banks should make no new loans to South Africa, including trade credits, and in the negotiations due by March 1990, banks should insist on rapid repayment of existing debt.**

There exists a broad consensus that the most effective pressure would be the application of comprehensive and mandatory sanctions by the UN Security Council. However, pending the adoption of such measures there are a range of sanctions which Britain could apply to bring its policy into line with the Commonwealth, Nordic and other European Community countries:

●**the introduction of appropriate legal controls to strengthen and enforce existing British measures, in particular the arms and oil embargos and a ban on new investment;**
●**a compulsory ban on all loans, trade credits and export credit guarantees;**
●**a compulsory ban on all 'high tech' and computer exports to South Africa;**
●**a compulsory ban on the importing of coal and agricultural products;**

The Cape is becoming one of the world's largest wine producers with regular tastings for foreign buyers.

Police confront workers as they leave Khotso House, the headquarters of the South African Council of Churches.

- an end to all promotion of trade and tourism to South Africa, and a suspension of air links;
- an urgent examination of the possibility of the sanction on gold.
- The British Government should also increase support for the members of SADCC and for an independent Namibia.

The moment is opportune. Pretoria is clearly heading in the wrong direction, and yet is under pressure

---

The moment is opportune. Pretoria is clearly heading in the wrong direction, and yet it is under pressure and shows signs of vacillating. Internal opposition, though repressed, remains high. The loss of diehard white support to the Conservative Party is a threat – but also an opportunity to override their preferences. The new openness of the Soviet Union, in southern Africa as elsewhere, diminishes the plausibility of the Communist bogey. The economy is clearly in long term decline, and business leaders are unhappy.

International pressure could tip the scales. Persuasion alone would not be enough: without real pressure the strategy of repressive reform becomes more viable, and Pretoria is confirmed on its present path. That path is emphatically not one of slow improvement for the majority. In May 1988, the South African Council of Churches and the Southern African Catholic Bishops' Conference sent to Britain the General Secretary of the SACC, the previous General Secretary of the SACC, a Roman Catholic Archbishop and Bishop, and the President of the Methodist Conference, to say:

". . . the Government of South Africa is closing the door to peaceful change and is making a clear choice for totalitariansim and violence. It is in the light of the dramatic deterioration of the South African situation that we have come to Europe."

Restrictive Measures implemented by Britain

1. Measures agreed at the Meeting of EC Foreign Ministers, September 1985.
    (i) A rigorously controlled embargo on exports of arms and para-military equipment to South Africa;
    (ii) A rigorously controlled embargo on imports of arms and para-military equipment from South Africa;
    (iii) A refusal to cooperate in the military sphere;
    (iv) The recall of military attaches accredited to South Africa and refusal to grant accreditation to military attaches from South Africa;
    (v) Discouraging cultural and scientific agreements except where these contribute towards the ending of apartheid or have no possible role in supporting it; and freezing of official contacts and international agreements in the sporting and security spheres;
    (vi) The cessation of oil exports to South Africa;
    (vii) The cessation of exports of sensitive equipment destined for the police and armed forces of South Africa;
    (viii) The prohibition of all new collaboration in the nuclear sector.

2. Measures agreed at the Commonwealth Heads of Government Meeting, Nassau, October 1985.
    (i) The strict enforcement of the mandatory Arms Embargo against South Africa;
    (ii) A re-affirmation of the Gleneagles declaration of 1977 which called upon Commonwealth members to take every practical step to discourage sporting contacts with South Africa;
    (iii) Agreement upon and commendation to other Governments of the adoption of the following further economic measures against South Africa:
        (A) A ban on all new government loans to the Government of South Africa and its agencies;

(B) A readiness to take unilaterally what action may be possible to preclude the import of Krugerrands;

(C) No government funding for trade missions to South Africa or for participation in exhibitions and trade fairs in South Africa;

(D) A ban on the sale and export of computer equipment capable of use by South African military forces, police or security forces;

(E) A ban on new contracts for the sale and export of nuclear goods, materials and technology to South Africa;

(F) A ban on the sale and export of oil to South Africa;

(G) A strict and rigorously controlled embargo on imports of arms, ammunition, military vehicles and para-military equipment from South Africa;

(H) An embargo on all military co-operation with South Africa;

(I) The discouragement of all cultural and scientific events except where these contribute towards the ending of apartheid or have no possible role in promoting it.

3. Measures which the UK agreed to implement following the Commonwealth Review Meeting, Marlborough House, August 1986.

(i) A voluntary ban on new investment in South Africa;

(ii) A voluntary ban on the promotion of tourism to South Africa;

(iii) The implementation of any EC decision to ban the import of coal, iron and steel and of gold coins from South Africa.

4. Measures agreed at the EC Meeting of Foreign Ministers, September 1986.

(i) A ban on imports of certain South African iron and steel;

(ii) A ban on the imports of certain South African gold coins;

(iii) A ban on certain new investment in South Africa.

Resolution on southern Africa approved by the British Council of Churches, 1989

SOUTHERN AFRICA

THE ASSEMBLY

receives and welcomes the background document presented to the Conference on Britain and Southern Africa held on February 28, 1989;[*]

endorses the Call to Action against Apartheid as presented in the Board report of the Division of International Affairs;[*]

confirms our solidarity with churches in South Africa as they continue their faithful witness for basic human rights;

condemns the continued repression of organisations and individuals striving for a democratic South Africa;

encourages HMG to increase development aid to the Front Line States and involvement in education for black South Africans, and the support of projects inside South Africa which fit the special criteria agreed between the European Community and the South African Churches;

welcomes the British Government's commitment to promote negotiation in South Africa along the lines proposed by the Commonwealth Eminent Persons Group in 1986;

believes that continuing international pressure is needed to secure the commitment of the South African Government to such negotiations;

urges HMG to adopt targeted, economic measures as part of such overall pressure in co-ordination with the Commonwealth and European Community (see appendix below);

and *believes* with the Commonwealth Eminent Persons Group that the objective of both international and internal pressure remains the dismantling of apartheid, the provision of freedom of association and debate, the removal of troops from the townships, the release of political prisoners and detainees, and the suspension of violence by all sides, so that a genuine constitutional debate about a democratic and non-racial future may begin.

Appendix:
Economic measures for consideration under clause eight above;

the introduction of appropriate legal controls to strengthen and enforce existing British measures, in particular the arms and oil embargoes and a ban on new investment;

a compulsory ban on all loans, trade credits and export credit guarantees;

a compulsory ban on all 'high tech' and computer exports to South Africa;

a compulsory ban on the importing of coal and agricultural products;

an end to all promotion of trade and tourism to South Africa, and a suspension of direct air links.

THE ASSEMBLY

requests UK banks to respond to the appeal of South African church leaders in connection with the 1990 negotiations for re-scheduling South Africa's debt, by making no new loans to South Africa while insisting on the rapid repayment of existing debt.

NAMIBIA:

THE ASSEMBLY

welcomes the promise of Namibian independence and is grateful to those who have persisted with appropriate pressure and negotiations over many years;

supports the call for all parties to observe the cease fire and for the UN to deploy sufficient forces to implement the agreed peace process.

* **Available from the British Council of Churches, Division of International Affairs, Africa Section, Inter-Church House, 35-41 Lower Marsh, London SE1 7RL. Tel: 01-620 4444.**

Bibliography

British Government Sources

British Overseas Trade Board, Speech by Sir James Cleminson, Chairman of BOTB, to the UK South Africa Association, October 13, 1988.

Foreign and Commonwealth Office, **British Policy towards South Africa,** 1988.

Howe, Rt Hon Sir Geoffrey, 'South Africa: No Easy Answers' in, **Perspectives on Africa,** Foreign and Commonwealth Office, 1988.

Overseas Development Administration, UK Aid Programme to Black South Africans, 1988.

Renwick, Sir Robin, Address at the **AGM of the Urban Foundation,** Johannesburg, August 17, 1988.

Thatcher, Rt Hon Mrs Margaret, Speech at Polish Government dinner, Warsaw, November 3 1988.

Further Reading

Anti-Apartheid Movement, **Selling Out to Apartheid: British Government Support for Trade with South Africa,** London, 1989.

British Council of Churches, **Whose Rubicon?: Report of a BCC delegation to South Africa,** 1986.

Catholic Institute for International Relations, South Africa church leaders confront the state: text of February 29, 1988 petition, 2 pp, 1988.

Chikane, Frank, **The Church's Prophetic Witness against the Apartheid System in South Africa** (February 25-April 8, 1988), SACC, Johannesburg, 1988.

Chikane, Frank, **The Churches and the South African Crisis,** CIIR, 1988.

Christian Aid, **Mozambique: Caught in the Trap,** London, 1988.

Commonwealth Committee of Foreign Ministers on Southern Africa, Concluding Statement of Second Meeting, Toronto, August 2-3, 1988, **Commonwealth News Release** 88/22, Commonwealth Secretariat, London.

Commonwealth Committee of Foreign Ministers on Southern Africa, South Africa's Relations with the International Financial System: **Report of the Inter-Governmental Group, Commonwealth Secretariat,** London, July 1988.

Commonwealth Eminent Persons Group, **Mission to South Africa,** London 1986.

de Gruchy, J, **The Church Struggle in South Africa,** 2nd edn, 1987.

Green, Reginald Herbold, 'Employment, Growth and Economic Policy in a Liberated South Africa: Some Issues and Reflections', in South Africa Economic Research and Training Project, **Beyond Apartheid,** Working Papers Vol 1, No 1, Amsterdam, 1988.

Hanlon, Joseph, **Beggar Your Neighbours,** Catholic Institute for International Relations/James Currey, 1986.

Hanlon, Joseph, and Omond, Roger, **The Sanctions Handbook,** Penguin, London, 1987.

Kairos, **The Kairos Document,** BCC/CIIR, 1985.

Leadership Publications, **Sanctions,** Cape Town, 1988.

Lipton, Merle, **Sanctions and South Africa,** Economist Intelligence Unit, London, 1988.

Makoni, Simba, SADCC Executive Secretary, Southern Africa: **Apartheid and Sanctions – The SADCC View,** Anti-Apartheid Movement, London, 1988.

Mare, Gerry and Hamilton, Georgina, **An Appetite for Power,** London, 1987.

Moorsom, Richard, **The Scope for Sanctions,** Catholic Institute for International Relations, London, 1986.

Orkin, Mark (ed), **Sanctions against Apartheid,** Cape Town, 1989.

Overseas Development Institute, **Sanctions and South Africa's Neighbours,** ODI Briefing Paper, May 1987.

Renwick, Robin, **Economic Sanctions,** Harvard Studies in International Affairs no. 45, Cambridge, Mass, 1981.

continued

Riddell, Roger C, 'New Sanctions against South Africa', in **Development Policy Review,** Vol 6, 1988.

Starnberger Institut, **The Economic Impact of Sanctions against South Africa,** Starnberg, 1987.

Swilling, Mark, and Phillips, Mark, **State Power in the 1980s: From Total Strategy to Counter-Revolutionary Warfare, Centre for Policy Studies,** University of the Witwatersrand, 1988.

UNICEF, **Children on the Front Line,** New York, 1987.

van Wyk, Chris, 'Facing the Nineties, Business amidst sanctions and disinvestment', in **South Africa International,** 19, July 1, 1988.

Whitehead, Deputy Secretary of State John C, **The Potential Impact of Imposing Sanctions against South Africa,** US Dept of State Current Policy No 1081, June 1988.

Wilson, Francis, and Ramphele, Mamphela, **Uprooting Poverty,** David Philip, Cape Town, 1989.

World Gold Commission, **The Case for a Gold Sanction,** London, 1989.